ALLSPORT
BOOK OF THE
DECADE
A MOMENT IN TIME

This edition produced by Ted Smart for

The Book People Ltd
Guardian House
Godalming Surrey GU7 2AE

ISBN 1-85613-001-0

The photographs in this book are courtesy of **Allsport**,
the World's leading sports photographic agency.

The publisher wishes to personally thank Darryl Ingham
and Christine Lalla whose professional approach and
knowledge of the library made this book possible.

For information about the photographs contact :

Allsport Photographic
3 Greenlea Park
Prince Georges Road
London SW19 2JD
081-685 1010

Manufactured in Spain

Produced by Ted Smart
Text and Captions by Rupert O. Matthews
Designed by Sara Cooper
Production Assistant : Seni Glaister

Page 1: Kevin Magee of Australia riding in the
1988 British Grand Prix.

Pages 2/3: Rick Mears powers ahead in the 1988
Indianapolis 500.

ALLSPORT

BOOK OF THE

DECADE

A MOMENT IN TIME

TED SMART

The decade of the 1980s was a dramatic and exciting one for the world of sports. World giants who had dominated the scene for years left active participation while new prodigies appeared on the world stage. Technical advances brought fresh challenges to the sportsmen and women of the world in their constant striving to be better than any before them.

In the tennis game the mighty Bjorn Borg announced that he would no longer be competing in the first class game, bowing out gracefully after a string of wins which placed him securely in the record books. He was followed off the world's tennis courts by Jimmy Connors, John Lloyd and Chris Evert. In their place arose Boris Becker and Pat Cash, two dashing young players and the glamorous Gabriella Sabatini.

Boxing saw the final retirement of Muhammed Ali who had dominated the heavyweight sport for over a decade and the rise of a new champion in the shape of Mike Tyson. While cricket saw Ian Botham achieve perhaps his finest performances.

But it was not only the high-profile characters which enlivened sports in the decade, there was also a fair degree of controversey. Indeed the decade kicked off with an international row of unprecedented proportions when the Moscow Olympics leapt into the headlines for all the wrong reasons. Just months before the Games were due to begin the Soviet Union invaded Afghanistan. Many western nations refused to send athletes to the Moscow Games in protest over the invasion. Four years later the Eastern Bloc countries boycotted the Los Angeles Olympics in retaliation. Thus two of the decades most prestigious sporting events were torn apart by forces far removed from sport.

Nor did the controversies stop there. The questions of drugs and amateurism both raised their heads as the 1980s progressed. The gold medal for the 100 metre sprint was stripped from the winner in the 1988 Seoul Olympics after he failed a drugs test. The taking of steroids and other performance-enhancing drugs was commonly suspected to be widespread in athletics, if not in other sports, and disputes frequently occurred.

The status of amateurism also came under fire. The ideal of part-time unpaid sportsmen which is upheld in many sports became increasingly rare in the 1980s. More and more sportsmen and women were full-time professionals in all but name. Some were maintained by the military while others survived as students or through sponsorship. Whether or not this constituted a breach of amateurism dominated discussions in many sporting bodies. Some decided to follow golf and tennis in allowing 'open' competitions while others resisted the impulse to change.

When a truly amateur sportsmen turned up at the 1988 Calgary Winter Olympics in the shape of the British ski-jumper Eddie 'The Eagle' Edwards he was so unusual that the true professionalism of sport was thrown into stark contrast. Eddie trained, if at all, in his spare time and came spectacularly last in his event. Perhaps his is the true amateurism which has been lost in sport.

Despite the upsets and disputes the world of sport remains extremely healthy. New world records continue to be set in many sports and new champions appear to dominate the world scene. If the world of sports has changed greatly during the 1980s, and it has, it can only be for the better as new levels of attainment are met and fresh triumphs recorded.

1. Simon Bruty

2. Mike Powell

3. Mike Neveux

6

4. Mike Powell

American football is a sport which has become increasingly popular during the 1980s. Always capable of pulling large crowds in the United States, the game caught on in Europe and Japan as top American teams played showpiece games. 1) A fraught moment in a tense cliff hanger of a game between the Buffaloes and the Oilers. The game ended in a narrow 34-30 victory for the buffaloes. 2) Redskin players grapple for the ball during their 42-10 trouncing of Denver in the XXII Superbowl. 3) A scrabble for a loose ball at the Browns Field Goal. 4) Doug Williams, the first black major league quarter back preparing to throw the ball as his team the Washington Redskins press ahead to scoop the XXII Superbowl. 5) Ken Bell of the Oilers in trouble during the XXII Superbowl in 1988. 6) Ricky Sanders of the Washington Redskins leaps over a diving tackle as he rushes the ball forward in the XXII Superbowl. 7) Anthony Toney of the Philadelphia Eagles rescues the ball from a mass of players, helping his team to a 17-5 victory over Phoenix in October 1989.

5. Mike Powell

7

The modern game of American Football had its origins in the rough and tumble games of football which were popular in medieval England. These early games also gave rise to European soccer and rugby, but in the United States developed into the thrilling sport of today. 1) Jim McMahon, the star quarter back of the Chicago Bears prepares for a mammoth throw which helped his team to a well-deserved 17-7 victory over Dallas. 2) Joe Montana of the San Francisco 49ers races with the ball in a contest with the Rams. 3) Herschel Wakler of the Vikings plunges into a mass of bodies in an heroic attempt to gain a few precious yards for his team in a tight match against the Packers in week 12 of the National Football League 1989-90 season. His efforts were to no avail for his team lost narrowly by 20 points to 19. 4) A tense moment for the players as Denver prepares to rush the Giants defence in the XXI superbowl. The efforts of Denver ended in disappointment for they were defeated convincingly 39-20. 5) Week 7 of the NFL 1989-90 season saw a gruelling match between the San Francisco 49ers and the New England Patriots which ended in a 37-20 victory for the 49ers.

1. Jonathan Daniel

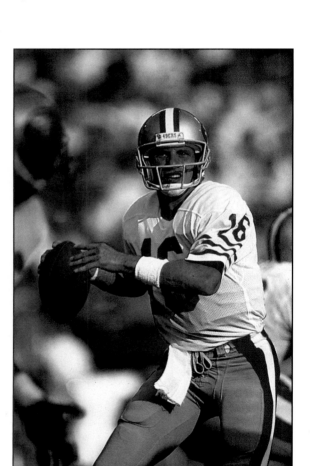

2. Mike Powell

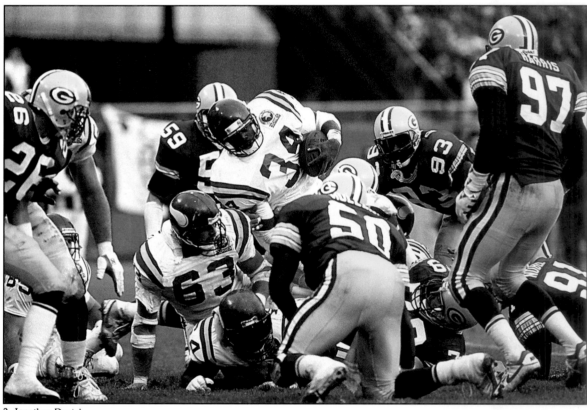

3. Jonathan Daniel

4. Mike Powell

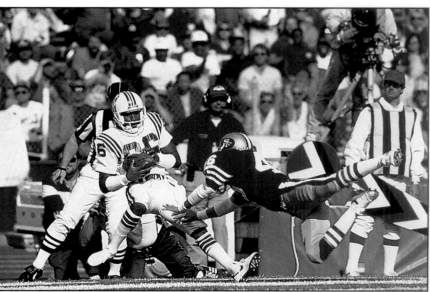

5. Otto Greule Jr.

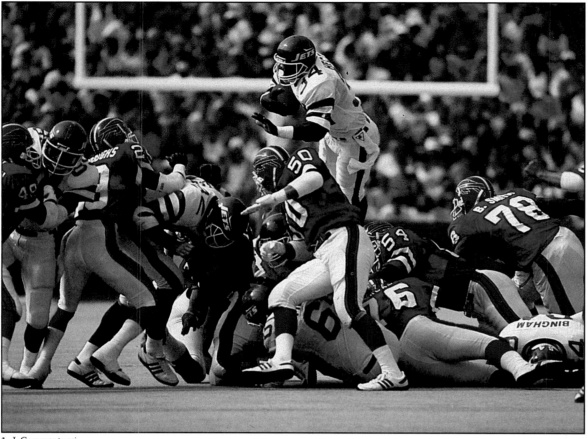

1. J. Commentucci

The game of American football as we know it today began in 1874 when Harvard played McGill University, Montreal, in the first game under the Harvard Rules. Previously games had been conducted under a number of loosely defined rules as the sport developed. Twenty one years later the game turned professional and the stage was set for the development of the multi-million dollar sport of today. 1) The Jets lose the ball in a ruck with the Buffaloes. 2) Gary Clark of the Washington Redskins grasps the ball in a spectacular diving catch as he helps his team to victory over Denver in the XXII Superbowl of 1988. 3) Joe Montana of the San Francisco 49ers hurls the ball forward moments before being dashed to the ground by the opposing Cincinnati Bengals. This incident took place during the XXIII Superbowl of 1989 which the 49ers went on to win. Joe Montana is widely recognised as possibly the best quarter back of the decade and exciting exploits such as this only further establish his reputation. 4) A spectacular tumble brings a New York Jets rush to a stop in a match against the Buffalo Bills. 5) A crushing tackle during Hawaii's Pro Bowl of 1987.

2. Mike Powell

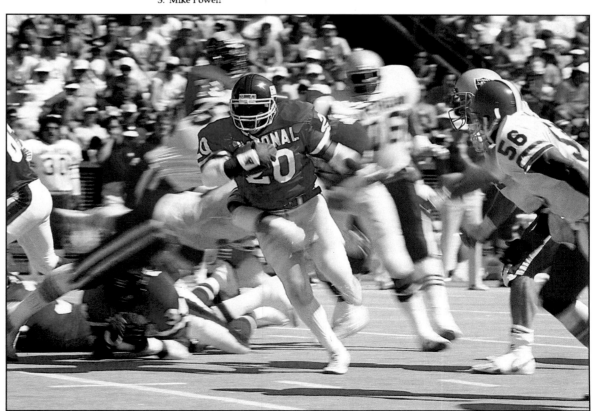

3. Mike Powell

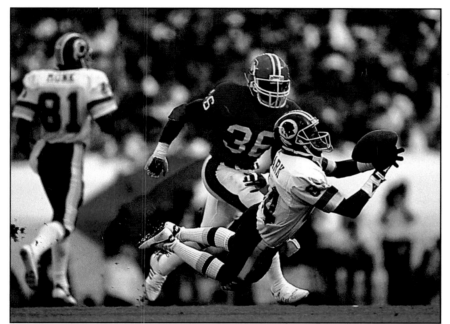

4. Trevor Jones

5. Mike Powell

1) The San Francisco 49ers rush a few valuable yards in a game with the Dolphins. 2) Walter Payton of the Chicago Bears in typically athletic poise as he charges forward. Payton is the record rusher of all time, covering a total of 16,726 yards in a professional career which ran from 1975 to 1988. One of his most astounding performances came early in his career when he rushed over 270 yards in a 1977 match against the Minnesota Vikings. 3) A desperate tackle during the narrowly fought match between the 49ers and Phoenix which ended in a 24-23 victory for Phoenix. 4) Ralf Mosiejenko kicks the ball forward for a massive gain during a tense match between the Raiders and the Chargers which resulted in a 17-13 Raiders victory. 5) John Elway of the Denver Broncos prepares to pass the ball during his teams 37-0 crushing of Phoenix in week 15 of the NFL 1989-90 season. John Elway has not been so successful at Superbowl. He has led his team in three Superbowl matches and has suffered three defeats.

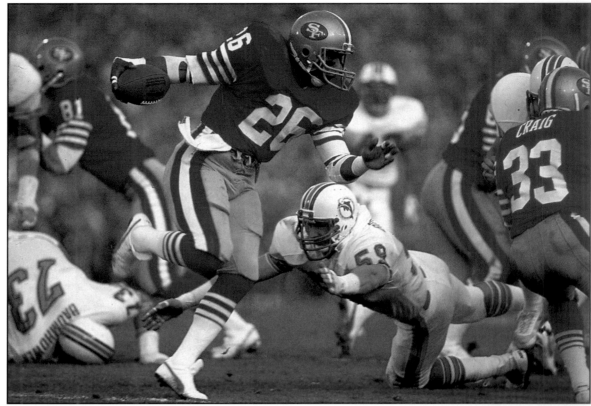

1. Tony Duffy

2. Tony Inzerillo

3. Mike Powell

4. Mike Powell

5. Stephen Dunn

1. Stephen Dunn

2. Tim de Frisco

3. Mike Powell

4. Mike Powell

5. Mike Powell

1) A Seattle player takes a spectacular tumble during a game with San Diego which ended in a 17-16 win for the Californian team. 2) Fans of the Denver Broncos celebrate as the opening game of the 1989-90 NFL comes to an end with their team obtaining a well-deserved 34-20 victory over the Chiefs. 3) The Giants prepare their defence with meticulous care during the 1987 Superbowl to stop any breakthrough. 4) Quarter back Rodney Peete races through open ground in the 1989 Rose Bowl, one of the premier matches of Collegiate football which are traditionally held on January 1st each year. 5) Karl Mecklenberg of the Denver Broncos in a bone-jarring collision in the 1987 match against Seattle. Mecklenberg is possibly the most formidable line backer of his generation, seemingly able to stop anything which comes his way.

1. Allsport

2. Tim de Frisco

Archery is one of the most ancient sports in the world. It originated so long ago that nobody is entirely certain when the sport began. The bow was certainly in use as a hunting weapon by about 15,000 years ago and it is reasonable to assume that these early archers engaged in competition with each other. The ancient Romans developed the war-bow into a sporting weapon around AD 300 but the sport died with the civilisation which bore it. The arrival of the longbow on the battlefields of Europe in the 13th century made archery a paramount hobby for would-be warriors. Kings encouraged their subjects to practise with organised competitions. The modern sport is directly descended from the medieval contests with at least one annual competition dating back to the 15th century. Modern weapons are far more sophisticated with stablisers and high-tech materials not available to medieval fighting archers in their battles.

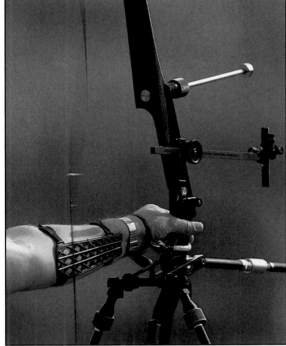

3. Yann Guichaoua

4. Allsport

5. Simon Bruty

6. Bob Martin

The modern sport of archery is administered by the Federation Internationale de Tir a l'Arc, now nearly 60 years old. It centres around a number of different rounds consisting of differing flights over various distances to different targets. The most often used rounds are the York, Hereford and FITA, the last being the standard of the Federation and the contest most used in Europe. It was only in 1931 that the sport became regularised on an international scale. Before that date different nations had held national championships under different rules, but there had been no mechanism for finding world champions. 1) Denise Parker of the United States of America shoots at the US Olympic Festival. 2) Dave Howell of Great Britain shooting freestyle at the World Games in 1985. 3) Field Archers inspect the results of their shooting during the 1985 World Games. 4) A line up of competition shooters in a women's event. 5) An anxious competitor pauses to use a pair of binoculars to check the accuracy of his flight during an international competition.

1. Damian Strohmeyer

2. Simon Miles

3. Simon Miles

4. Don Morley

5 Russell Cheyne

1. Steve Powell

2. Tony Duffy

3. Tony Duffy

4. Tony Duffy

5. Steve Powell

Facing page: The Los Angeles Olympic Games of 1984 saw the gathering together of arguably the three finest middle distance runners Britain has ever produced, certainly the greatest of their generation. From left to right the three white-vested athletes are Steve Ovett, Steve Cram and Seb Coe. At the time of the Los Angeles Olympics, Seb Coe held two world records. He had run the 800 metres in 1 minute 41.73 seconds at Florence, Italy in June 1981. One month later he had broken the 1500 metre record with a time of 2 minutes 12.18 seconds at Oslo. Within a year of the games Steve Cram set his own world record in the mile with a magnificent time of 3 minutes 46.32 seconds in Oslo. 1) Steve Cram breaks into a grin as he breasts the tape to take first place in the 1500 metres at the 1983 World Championships. 2) British athlete Alan Wells powers to victory in the 100 metres hurdles at the 1980 Moscow Olympics. 3) Seb Coe spreads his arms to embrace victory as he takes the gold medal for the 1500 metres at the 1980 Moscow Olympics. 4) Steve Ovett, after racing in the 1500 metres at Moscow. 5) Seb Coe gestures to friends in the crowd seconds after winning the gold medal for the 1500 metres at the Los Angeles Olympics.

1. Steve Fowell

2. Tony Duffy

3. Tony Duffy

4. Joe Patronite

The Seoul Olympics of 1988 were the first
attended by national teams of both Eastern and
Western block countries after the political
disputes which surrounded the Moscow and Los
Angeles Olympics. They were not, however, free
of controversy. 1, 3, 4 & 6) As widely predicted
the 100 metre sprint was won by Canada's Ben
Johnson in startling form which set a new record.
5) Johnson celebrating his win beside the maple
leaf flag. The victory was, however, disallowed
when Johnson failed a drugs test. It was later
claimed that he had inadvertently taken the drug
in minute quantities, but the disqualification
stood and the record was disallowed.

5. Bob Martin

6. Agence Vandystadt

3. Tony Duffy

4. Gerard Vandystadt

5. Bob Martin

6. Tony Duffy

7. Tony Duffy

1) The great Carl Lewis of the United States of America racing for take off at the long jump plank. To date no athlete has managed to outreach the massive leap of 29 feet 2 inches made by Robert Beaman of the United States at the Mexico Olympics of 1968. 2) Steve Cram racing in second place during the 1988 British Olympic Trials. The method by which an Olympic team is selected has recently come under criticism. Some commentators hold that inclusion should be based simply on performance at the Trials. Others hold that it is unfair to expect known high performers to compete, and possibly peak out, before the main event. Whether top sportsmen and women should be included automatically or not is a continuing debate. 3) Seb Coe, Steve Cram and Steve Ovett running together in the final of the 1500 metres at the 1980 Moscow Olympics. 4) Bradley Cooper of the Bahamas winding himself up for a discus throw at the Oslo Games of 1987. The discus dates back to the original Olympics held by the Ancient Greeks, although the origins of the sport remain obscure. 5) Ed Moses of the USA in action at the 1987 World Championships in Rome. 6) Carl Lewis shows his patriotism at the 1984 Los Angeles Olympics. 7) Said Aouita of Morocco at the 1988 Seoul Olympics at which time he was holder of the 1500 metres, 2,000 metres and 5,000 metres world records.

1. Bob Martin

2. Billy Stickland

3. Gerard Vandystadt

4. Felix Oppenheim

5. Mike Powell

4) Like many modern field sports, pole vaulting is a highly stylised form of what was once an essential skill. Many people have seen the origins of pole vaulting in the ditch vaulting of the Netherlands. Natives of Holland used to carry long poles with which they vaulted over the many water-filled ditches of the country. Today pole vaulters aim for height, not length. 1) Sergei Bubka of the USSR competing at Oslo in 1987. A few months later Bubka set a new world record of 6.06 metres (19 feet 10 inches). 2) Sigfried Hentz of East Germany at the 1987 World Championships in Rome. 3) Disaster strikes Daley Thompson at the pole vault. Thompson is possibly the greatest living athlete. His spectacular all round performances in the decathlon with an unbeaten 8847 points in the 1984 Olympics show him to be a master of many disciplines including shot-putting (6) and the long jump (7). 5) Greg Tafralis of the USA.

6. Steve Powell

Yann Guichaoua

1. Gray Mortimore

2. Gray Mortimore

3 Steve Powell

4. Gerard Vandystadt

5. Tony Duffy

6. Bob Martin

Facing page: The start of the 100 metres final at the 1984 Los Angeles Olympics. The discus event was adopted into the modern Olympics direct from the ancient games where it was an important event. Homer mentions the Greek heroes engaging in discus events in their spare time during the siege of Troy, but the exact origins of the sport are obscure. It has been suggested that the discus was originally of stone and was used as a weapon. The shape and spinning action of the discus making it fairly accurate at long ranges and capable of inflicting a painful wound. 1) W. Schmidt at the Helsinki Games of 1989. 4) Olav Jensen of Norway. 5) Torsten Voss of East Germany letting fly a spectacular throw at the 1987 World Championships in Rome. 2) Vladimir Melihov of the USSR in the triple jump event of the World Junior Championships in 1988. 3) Daley Thompson powering his way to complete the 110 metre hurdles in 14.3 seconds as part of his record breaking decathlon of 1984. 6) Sigfried Wentz of West Germany pole vaulting at the 1987 World Championships in Rome.

3. Tony Duffy

4. Bob Martin

5. Tony Duffy

6. Steve Powell

7. Bob Martin

1) Dietmar Mogenberg clearing the high jump using the style known as the Fosbury Flop, named after the American sportsman who developed the backward flip in the late 1960s. Prior to that date most jumpers had used a scissors style. 2) Daley Thompson launching himself into the pole vault, one of the ten decathlon events. 3) The change-over during the 4x100 metres relay race at the 1988 Seoul Olympics when the world record of 37.8 seconds set at the Los Angeles games was narrowly missed. 4) Said Aouita, one of the greatest long distance runners of the 1980s at the Helsinki Games of 1987. 5) The great Russian hammer thrower Yuri Sedykh at the 1988 Seoul Olympics where he failed to break his own world record of 86.7 metres (284 feet 7 inches) which he set two years earlier in Stuttgart. 6) Carl Lewis powering ahead to take the United States 4x100 metres relay team to gold medals a the 1984 Los Angeles Olympics and a new world record. 7) Grigory Yegorov of the USSR pole vaulting at the Cologne Games of 1989.

3. Tony Duffy

Both the javelin and shot putting have military origins. Javelin throwing is fairly obviously descended from ancient spear-throwing techniques while shot putting had its origins in soldiers throwing cannonballs for sport. 1) Stephanie Hightowers leaping to victory in the hurdles at the 1987 World Championships in Rome. 2) Petra Felke of East Germany at the Stockholm Games of 1988. 3) Jackie Joyner-Kersee preparing to throw the javelin at the 1987 Rome World Championships. The following year she set a new world record of 7215 points for the event, establishing herself as the best all-round sportswoman of the decade. 4) Britain's Lesley-Anne Skeete racing to second place in the 100 metre hurdles at the 1989 Girobank Games. 5) America's Jane Frederick braces herself to put the shot in the heptathlon. 6) Jackie Joyner-Kersee leaps for the long jump section of the heptathlon a the Seoul Olympics. 7) Tina Lillak of Finland. 8) Florence Griffith-Joyner, or Flo-Jo, at the 1987 Rome World Championships before going on to greater fame at the Seoul Olympics.

4 Gray Mortimore

5. Jean-Marc Barey

6. Tony Duffy

7. Tony Duffy

8. Billy Stickland

Athletics as we know it today is a more or less conscious borrowing from ancient Greece. Many of the events competed in today were also played over 2,000 years ago. The motive for the games has, however, changed. To the ancient Greeks they had strong religious overtones with contests being held to honour the gods. The winners were believed to be those who were specially favoured by the Olympian gods, and therefore acquired a slight tinge of sacredness themselves. Today most athletes compete for more worldly reasons. 1) The 4.100 metre race at the 1987 World Championships in Rome. 2) The East German heptathlon team of Behmer, John and Schulz stays close together in the 800m race section of the heptathlon at the 1988 Seoul Olympics. 3) The Canadian 4x400 metres relay team pose for photographers before racing in the Seoul Olympics. 4) A forlorn athlete in the rain at the 1987 Rome World Championships. 5) Florence Griffith-Joyner praying as she waits to receive the baton as the third racer in the 4x100 metre at the 1988 Seoul Olympics. The prayers were answered and Flo-Jo added another gold medal to her growing collection. 6) Nelli Cooman of the Netherlands tenses herself before settling down on the blocks a the 1987 Rome World Championships.

1. Jean-Marc Barey

2. Gray Mortimore

3. Gray Mortimore

4. Gerard Vandystadt

5. Gerard Vandystadt

6. Gerard Vandystadt

1. Rick Stewart

1) Perhaps the most controversial race of the 1980s came at the 1984 Los Angeles Olympics. Zola Budd, here wearing number 151, competed for Britain although she had been born in South Africa. Her change of nationality was seen by many to be an attempt to evade the sporting sanctions imposed on South Africa. World opinion split dramatically into those who vented anti-South African feelings on Budd and those who felt she should be given a chance to race. The attitude of Mary Decker, wearing 373, was never in doubt. She wanted to beat Budd to the gold medal. In the long awaited race the two runners collided, sending Decker sprawling and Budd losing her balance and place so that neither won the coveted medal. 2) Florence Griffith-Joyner prays before the 4x400 metres at the Seoul Olympics. She failed to win a fourth gold medal and had to be content with a silver. 3) Marita Koch of East Germany winning the gold medal for the 400 metres at the 1980 Moscow Olympics. 4) Florence Griffith-Joyner winning the 100 metres at Seoul and (5) celebrating moments later.

2. Tony Duffy

3. Don Morley

4. Mike Powell

5. Mike Powell

The extremely masculine sport of Australian rules football is largely confined to the nation which created it. Unlike most other football games it is played on an oval pitch which has four goal posts at each 'end'. Scoring depends on propelling the ball between the posts, with different points for different positions. The game is played with great fervour and passion by large men, and it is not unusual for fights to break out between players, entire teams being involved on occasion. In some ways the Australian rules football is closer to the original medieval sport than other forms of football. In the middle ages games were played annually between rival towns, or between sections of the same town. Often teams consisted of many hundreds of players as all able-bodied men turned out to defend the civic honour. Goals were local landmarks, such as church doors or bridges, and rules were almost non-existent. It has been quipped that the only rule was that deadly

1. Russell Cheyne

2. Chris Raphael

3. Russell Cheyne

4. K. Rainsbury

5. Russell Cheyne

6. Russell Cheyne

1. Chris Raphael

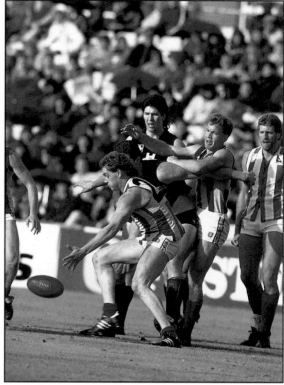

2. Russell Cheyne

3. Russell Cheyne

4. K. Rainsbury

5 Bob Martin

weapons were not to be used, except by prior arrangement. In most areas the old games have been suppressed by local authorities which became increasingly worried about the disorder and violence which surrounded the game. Possibly the oldest game, that of Kingston-upon-Thames in Surrey, was banned in the late 19th century. Attempts have been made to introduce Australian rules football to other nations but these have been only marginally successful. The Australian lager brewers Fosters have sponsored exhibition matches at the Kennington Oval in London in both 1987, when Carlton beat Melbourne (page 30 pictures 1, 2, 3, 5 and page 31 pictures 1, 2, 5), and in 1989, when Melbourne defeated the Essendon Bombers (Page 30 picture 6 and Page 31 picture 3). The VFL Grand Final in 1987 was played between Hawks and Brereton (page 30 picture 4 and page 31 picture 4).

1. Tony Duffy

2. Bob Martin

3. John Gichigi

4. Bob Martin

5. John Gichigi

The game of badminton is of modern origin, developing on the Badminton estates of the Dukes of Beaufort about 150 years ago. The combination of speed, athleticism, strength and delicacy required by the game make it far more demanding than it at first appears. 1) Morten Frost of Denmark competing in the Yonex All-England Championship of 1989, the premier contest of the badminton world. Frost is probably the greatest exponent of the game playing today and has a string of titles to his credit. 2) Norah Perry and Gillian Gilks. 3) Mike Tredgett. 4) The star doubles players the Sidek Brothers. 5) Tian Bingyi leaps for a stroke in the 1989 Yonex All-England Championship. 6) The British doubles players, Tredget and Stevens. 7) Nora Perry and M Tredget playing in the mixed doubles event. 8) Darren Hall of England running to reach a shuttle during the 1989 Oracle English Badminton Championships. 9) Tsun and Adahjudi, two of several great Indonesian players to dome on to the international scene in the 1980s. 10) The British player Chapman recovers from playing a shot.

6. Tony Duffy

7. Bob Martin

8. Gray Mortimore

9. Tony Duffy

10. Bob Martin

Hot air ballooning is a relaxing and gentle sport which has many exponents. 1) A skirt of material fixed around the burner to funnel hot air into the balloon. 2) Balloons lift off at La Clusaz in France. Because the lift for the balloon depends upon the difference in temperature between air inside and outside the balloon, the most spectacular flights are often made in winter. 3) Many balloonists carry advertising on their craft in order to fund the sport. 4) Ballooning over Capadocia in Turkey. 5) The balloon in the shape of a chateau shown here is owned by a French aristocrat and is a perfect copy of his country mansion. 7 & 9) Balloon preparing to lift off from Rocamadour in France. 6 & 8) The largest number of balloon to take off together was 128 at the Bristol International Balloon festival in August 1987.

2. Jean-Marc Barey

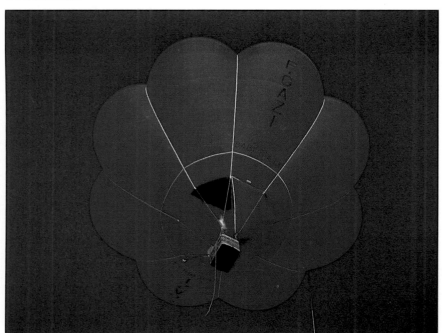
1. G. Bordessoule

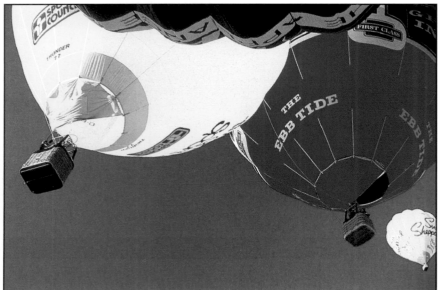
3. Pascal Rondeau

4. Vania Fine

5. Didier Page

6. Pascal Rondeau

7. Agence Vandystadt

8. Oli Tennent

9. Agence Vandystadt

1. John Hayt

2. John Hayt

3. Mike Powell

4. John Hayt

The game of baseball originated in the United States early last century, but it can trace its origins back to the country game of rounders played in Britain. The modern form of the game was first established by Alexander Cartwright of Hoboken, New Jersey, in 1846 and the rules have remained largely unchanged since. These rules are far more complicated than those of the rustic game which involve little more than hitting the ball and running around the bases. 1) Jason Thompson swings his bat behind him as he cracks a ball over the head of the pitcher. 2) Flannery dives to reach second base while Kemp waits in vain for the ball to reach him first. 3) Kirk Mcaskill winds himself up while eyeing the batter prior to a scorching pitch. 4) Juan Beniquez of the Angels sprints for first base after making contact with a pitch and sending the ball skywards. 5) A dramatic moment in a match between the Red Sox and the Angels results in a difficult decision for the umpire.

5. Stephen Dunn

1) Randy Bush prepares to bat. 2) Willie McGee slides for base while Mariano Dunean tries to beat him to it during a tightly fought final play off between the Dodgers and the Cardinals. 3) Stewart Cliburn lets fly one of his famous pitches from the pitchers mound. 4) Darryl Strawberry of the Mets lifts his foot off the ground as he puts all his efforts into swinging at an approaching ball. 5) Danny Tartabull of the Kansas City Royals in the act of hitting a home run. The ability to hit home runs is that most highly prized among batters. By the time he retired from Major League baseball in 1976 Hank Aaron had achieved an unsurpassed 755 home runs. However, not even he could outdo the legendary 'Babe' Ruth who played Major League between 1914 and 1938. In the course of his career he hit 714 home runs. Though less than the total of Hank Aaron, Babe Ruth's total was produced from far fewer times at bat. No batter has yet beaten Babe's record of hitting a home run from 8.5% of times at bat. 6) Candelaria slides forward to deliver an unplayable pitch.

1. John Hayt

2. Mike Powell

3. John Hayt

4. Tony Inzerillo

5. Tony Inzerillo

6. John Hayt

B. Schwartzman

1. Rick Stewart

2. John Hayt

3. Jonathan Daniel

4. T. G. Higgins

5. John Hayt

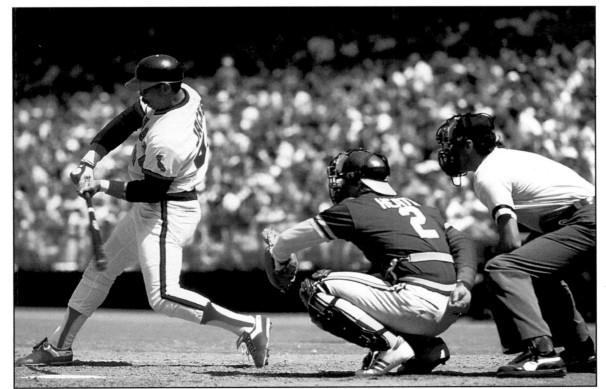

6. John Hayt

Facing page: David Cone of the Mets prepares for a pitch. Though there have been many great pitchers this century, none has beaten the 511 successful games pitched by Denton Young between 1890 and 1911. 1) Sammy Kalifa of Pittsburgh takes a dramatic dive in an attempt to catch the ball and run out an opponent. 2) Pete Rose who holds the Major League record for the most base hits in a career with a massive 4,256 attained during a 23 year career which ended in 1986. 3) Lancaster of the Chicago Cubs delivers a lightning pitch. 4) A jubilant group of Mets players celebrating a narrowly gained victory over the Boston Red Sox with a score line of 4-3. The result remained in doubt right up to the last ball and the release of pent up emotion brought the Mets together in a flamboyant display of success. 5) Pedro Guerrero of Los Angeles sends a ball flying deep into the outfield before setting off to reach 2nd base. 6) Reggie Jackson misses a low pitch on his second strike at bat.

1. Mike Powell

2. Mike Powell

3. Jonathan Daniel

4. Mike Powell

Though there have been many games around the world which centred around propelling a ball through a hoop or into an elevated container, basketball as we know it today did not come into existence until the end of the last century. 1) Erwin 'Magic' Johnson of the Los Angeles Lakers. Johnson is reckoned to be the most valuable National Basketball League player of the 1980s. His almost unfailing successes on the court have ensured him a place in basketball history books. 2) Harold Pressley of Sacramento races forward with the ball. 3) Michael Jordan of the Chicago Bulls dodges past a less nimble-footed opponent. 4) Walter Davis of Phoenix leaps above the Lakers defence to score much needed points. 5) Patrick Ewing of the New York Knicks pauses during a match against the Lakers. 6) Barkley and Worthy contest a high-leaping ball. 7) James 'Twiggy' Sanders of the Harlem Globetrotters. The Globetrotters are among the most popular teams in the world for they concentrate as much on clowning and entertaining the crowd as they do on scoring points. 8) An unusual picture taken from above the basket as the ball flies unerringly to score. 9) Mychal Thompson of the Lakers makes a scoring throw against Phoenix.

5. Mike Powell

6. Stephen Dunn

7. Mike Powell

8. Rick Stewart

9. Mike Powell

1. Steven E. Sutton

2. Steven E. Sutton

3. Steven E. Sutton

4. Steven E. Sutton

5. Steven E. Sutton

The modern sport of speed roller skating was not made possible until the 1860s when the stable four-wheeled skate was invented by Jim Plimpton of New York. Before that time various attempts to introduce a form of skating which was not dependent on winter ice were not particularly successful. Skates with two wheels set fore and aft were found to be dangerously unstable while other configurations failed to give the manoeuvrability required. Modern racing rinks have been the site of many exciting and thrilling contests with skaters achieving speeds of anything up to 43 kilometres per hour (26 miles per hour). This competition was fought out between the Bombers and Express teams in 1986.

6. Steven E. Sutton

Bi-cross is a thrilling modern derivation of cycling, a sport over a century old. The appearance of the extremely tough and robust bicycles known as BMX in the early 1980s made it possible for even those with a limited pocket to indulge in cross country bicycle racing over tracks and obstacles which would shake conventional bicycles to pieces in a short time. The exciting and demanding sport quickly gained a following, with teenage boys being particularly keen to take up the challenge. The addition of glamorous and colourful suits and helmets added to the appeal of the sport which quickly caught on with adults. Though only loosely organised, the sport established links on an international scale with individuals and teams from various nations travelling to take on rivals elsewhere.

1. Jean-Marc Loubat

2. Felix Oppenheim

3. Pascal Rondeau

4. Agence Vandystadt

5. Pascal Rondeau

2. Mike Powell

1. Gerard Vandystadt

3. Mike Powell

4. Gerard Vandystadt

5. Bernard Asset

6. Yann Guichaoua

7. Gerard Vandystadt

8. Allsport

9. Guido Benetton

10. Yann Guichaoua

1) The East German no.1 4-man bobsleigh team which took the silver medal at the 1988 Winter Olympics. 2) The New Zealand no.1 4-man bobsleigh team speeds round a high-banked corner at the 1988 Winter Olympics. 3) The distinctively coloured Austrian no.1 4-man bobsleigh at the 1988 Calgary Winter Olympics. 4) The Portuguese 4-man bobsleigh team at the 1988 Winter Olympics. 5) The Swiss 4-man bobsleigh team races to victory at the 1987 World Championships held at St Moritz. The driver, Ralf Pichler, and his brakeman, Celest Poltera, are possibly the best in the world. 6) The British 4-man bobsleigh team at the 1989 World Championships at Cortina d'Ampezzo. 7) The Swiss no.2 4-man bobsleigh team of Hiltebrand, Fehlman, Fassbind and Kiser at the 1988 Winter Olympics. 8) Jamaica is not known for its winter sports, but it fielded a 4-man bobsleigh team at the 1988 Winter Olympics. The gallant quartet worked with near-obsolete equipment and ended up in this crash. 9) The 2-man bobsleigh event at the 1988 Winter Olympics. 10) The British no.2 team of Phipps, Leeson, Richards and Rattigan at the 1989 World Championships.

1 & 2) The bout between Muhammed Ali and Larry Holmes in 1980 was held in Las Vegas and ended in defeat for Muhammed Ali, ending his 20-year long dominance of heavyweight boxing. 3) Muhammed Ali lets fly at Dunn but fails to make contact, in a successful defence of his world championship in 1975. 4) Larry Holmes and Leon Spinks during their 1986 fight which Holmes won. 5) George Foreman struggles unsuccessfully to rise after being sent sprawling by Muhammed Ali in their fight of 30th October 1974. Ali had earlier been stripped of his world title by the authorities but won it back in convincing style in this bout. 6) Muhammed Ali dodges a blow from Leon Spinks in September 1978 before going on to win the world heavyweight title for a record-breaking third time.

1. Steve Powell

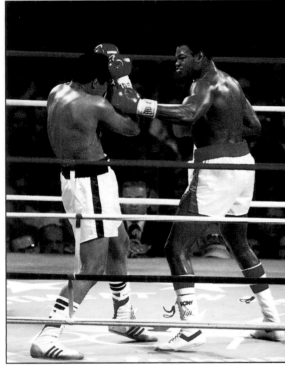

2. Steve Powell

3. Steve Powell

4. R. Mackson

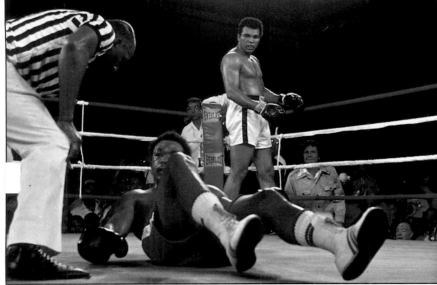

5. Allsport

6. Allsport

1. Patty Wood

2. Holly Stein

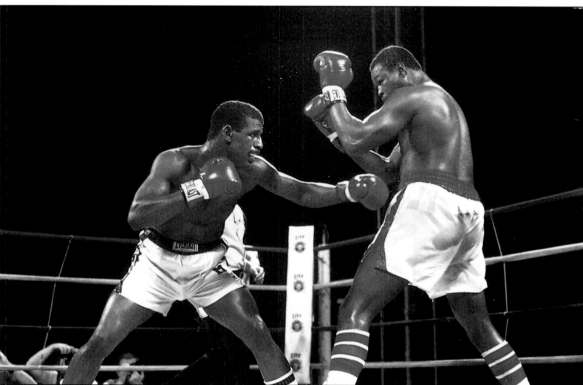

4 R. Mackson

3 Holly Stein

5. Dan Helms

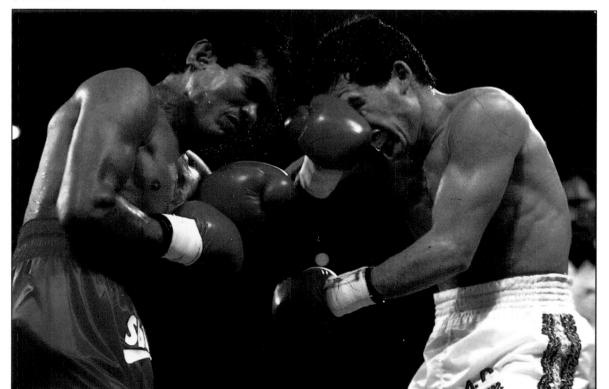

6 Holly Stein

The world heavyweight championship has been the most popular of boxing events since the first bout under modern rules when Gentleman Jim Corbett beat John Sullivan after 21 rounds in 1892. 1) A brooding George Foreman poses before the American flag before attempting to recapture the World Heavyweight Championship which he had lost to Muhammed Ali in 1974. Foreman was hoping to beat the record set in 1951 by Joe Walcott who was the oldest man to win the heavyweight championship aged 37 years, but he failed in his attempt. 2) Larry Holmes lands a crushing blow on Cooney during his victorious bout of 1982. 3) Larry Holmes and Leon Spinks sparring during their battle of 1986 which resulted in a victory for Larry Holmes. 4) Larry Holmes steps back to evade a punch from Cooney during the early stages of their 1982 fight. Larry Holmes and his support team being introduced to the expectant crowd before his 1982 struggle against Cooney. 6) The two hispanic boxers Chavez and Ramirez struggle with close in blows.

1. Steve Powell

2. Steve Powell

4. John Gichigi

3. Mike Powell

2) Alan Minter in determined mood enters the ring for his 1980 fight against 'Marvellous' Martin Hagler. 1) The much battered Alan Minter in the closing stages of his fight with Hagler. The fight was highly charged with emotion even before the two boxers met with Minter boasting that no black was going to take his title away from him. After suffering severe cuts in the opening rounds, Minter was judged unfit to continue by the referee who stopped the fight. The decision sparked a riot in the crowd which had been determined to see their hero defeat Hagler. 3) Barry McGuigan warms up for his Las Vegas fight against Cruz in June 1986. 4) Harold Graham celebrates his taking of the middleweight title by showing the highly-prized belt to the crowd. 5) The welterweight title fight between Lloyd Honeyghan and Don Curry in 1986 which was won by Lloyd Honeyghan.

5. Chris Cole

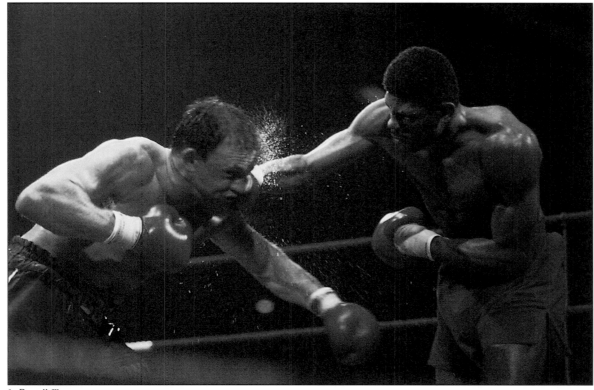

1. Russell Cheyne

1) Sibson misjudges a blow aimed at Tate during the tenth round of their 1988 fight, and is met by a smashing blow to the jaw. The punch floored Sibson who failed to regain his feet within the stipulated ten seconds and so lost the contest. 2) Watson and Nigel Benn jostle for position during their 1989 eliminator for the British title. The fight ended in the sixth round when Watson punched Benn to the canvas. 3) Smith tries to dodge a blow from Mike Tyson, but to no avail for he lost the bout. Tyson is without doubt the great heavyweight boxer of the decade, dominating the sport in much the same way as did Muhammed Ali in the 1960s and 1970s, though without Ali's gift for self-publicity epitomised by the famous phrase 'float like a butterfly, sting like a bee'. 4) Sims lands a telling blow on Duran during their fight held at Caesar's Palace Casino in Las Vegas, a much-favoured venue for important fights. 5) 'Marvellous' Martin Hagler throws a punch at Thomas 'Hitman' Hearnes during his successful bout for the middleweight championship.

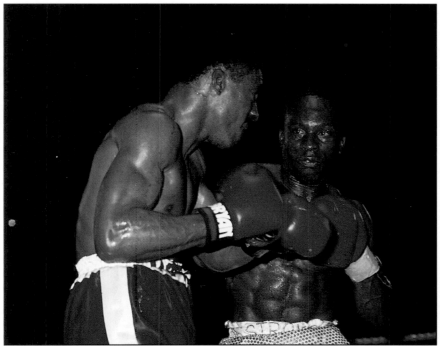

2. John Gichigi

4 Allsport

5. David Cannon

3. Holly Stein

1 & 6) Mike Tyson battles with Tony Tucker for the undisputed heavyweight championship of the world. Tyson had earlier won the WBA title by beating 'Bonecrusher' Smith in March 1987 and took the WBC title from Trevor Berbick in November 1986. 4) In 1989 Tyson faced a challenge to his undisputed title from the British boxer Frank Bruno who had established a growing reputation through victories over men such as Phil Brown (7). Frank Bruno was exceptionally popular in Britain, not only as a successful boxer but as a personality in his own right. His humorous exchanges with sports commentators caused much amusement in sporting circles while his engaging charm gave him star status in many commercials. The fight ended in a crushing defeat for Frank Bruno at the hands of Tyson who has yet to lose a professional match. 2) Martin Hagler fighting his way to victory over Duran in 1983. 3) Martin Hagler met Sugar Ray Leonard on 6th April 1987 for the middleweight title but lost on points. 5) Sibson collapses backwards after being struck by Andreis. He failed to recover within the ten seconds.

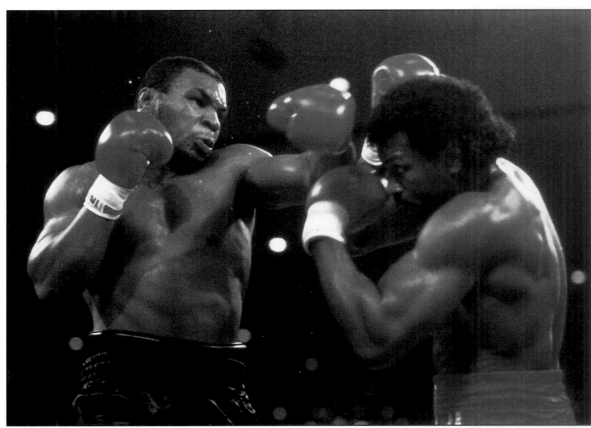

1. Bob Martin

2. Allsport

3. Dan Helms

4. Bob Martin

5. Chris Cole

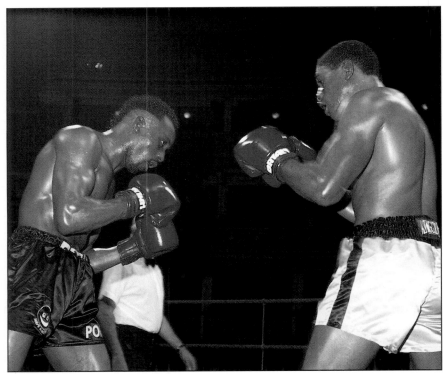

1. John Gichigi

2. Russell Cheyne

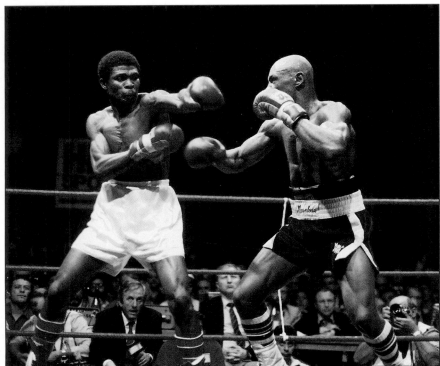

3. Tony Duffy

4. Russell Cheyne

6

1) Nigel Benn, who goes by the colourful name of 'the Dark Destroyer' crouches preparatory to delivering a blow at Miller. 2 & 7) The Dark Destroyer, Nigel Benn, tackle Umaru Sanda, landing a series of telling blows. 3) 'Marvellous' Martin Hagler defeating Obel. 4 & 5) Frank Bruno successfully takes on Joe Bugner in 1987. Bugner was originally born in Hungary but moved to Britain at an early age and went on to take the British heavyweight title from Henry Cooper in 1971. His comeback sixteen years later was launched from Australia where he had lived for some years. He appeared on newsreels against a backdrop of outback scenery and wearing typically Australian outback clothing. Despite long and strenuous training by Joe Bugner most commentators considered that his glory days were passed and he duly lost to Frank Bruno. Bugner then announced that he was giving up boxing to pursue an acting career. 5) Frank Bruno rides a punch from Tim Witherspoon during his first attempt at the world heavyweight title in 1986. Bruno lost the bout to Witherspoon who lost his title soon afterwards.

5. Bob Martin

7

1. Bob Martin

2. Bob Martin

The modern kayak is made of fibre-glass and other synthetic materials, but it is based upon the tradition craft of the Greenland Eskimos. The light, double bowed craft were made of seal skin stretched over whalebone and were used when the eskimos were hunting marine mammals or fishing in the chill northern waters. 1) Vincent Radoux of Belgium during the 1987 World Championships. 2) The French team of Calori and Calori plunge through the spray during the two man kayak wildwater competition at the 1987 World Championships. 3) Esa Veijola of Finland struggles to keep his craft upright during the one man kayak wildwater competition at the 1987 World Championships. 4) The inherent strength and stability of the kayak is shown in the wildwater events. Facing page: A canoeist celebrates after tackling the Record Descent.

3. Bob Martin

4. Bob Martin

International canoeing is divided into a number of disciplines each demanding different skills and techniques. The Canadian canoe is open at the top, unlike the kayak, and is propelled by the canoeist kneeling upright and wielding single-bladed paddles. Canadian canoeing is usually engaged in by teams rather than individuals and the courses are often long distance runs along rivers. The enclosed kayak is usually manned by one or two crew and may be used in any one of three events. The speed races are usually held across relatively flat water and judged on the time taken. Slalom, as the name suggests, involves the canoe weaving between poles dangling over the water. Slalom events are usually held on rougher water. Most spectacular of all are the wild water races. As their name suggests these are races run over rapids and turbulent streams. The greatest hazard of all is the Saut de Chute at the Parc d'Ordesa in France (6 & 8) which is a sheer waterfall 28 metres (90 feet) tall plunging into a deep pool.

1. P. Blondel

2. Agence Vandystadt

3. Agence Vandystadt

7

4. P. Blondel

5. Agence Vandystadt

6. Laurent Chevallier

8

1. Adrian Murrell

2. Adrian Murrell

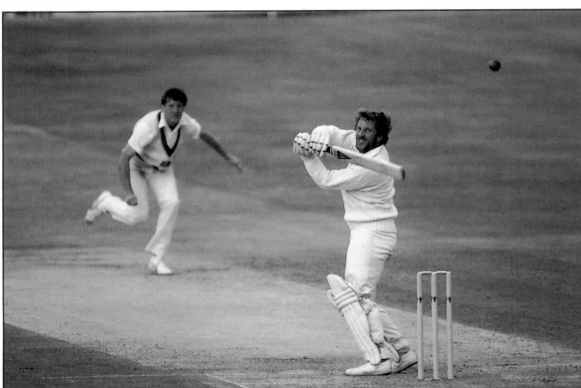

3. Adrian Murrell

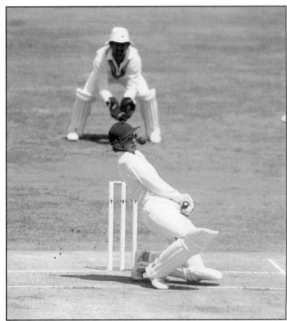

4. Adrian Murrell

1) Dennis Lillee delivering one of his scorching fast balls at England during the 1981 Ashes series. 2) Ian Botham, the English cricket sensation of the 1980s, celebrates taking yet another New Zealand wicket, giving him the record for wickets in a test match against New Zealand. 3) Ian Botham knocks a ball from Lawson towards the boundary during his phenomenal test innings at the Leeds Ashes Test of 1981. 4) David Gower bends back to avoid a ball during the Third Test against India in 1986. 5) Allan Lamb hooks at a ball during a match between Worcestershire and Northamptonshire. 6) Geoff Marsh of Australia ducks to avoid a bouncer delivered by test newcomer Devon Malcolm during the Fifth Ashes Test in 1989. 7) A scramble among the fielders during the Fifth Test between England and Australia at Edgbaston in 1985. 8) An appeal by Defratas for the wicket of Hooper during the Fifth Test between England and the West Indies at the Oval in 1988, but the umpire kept his finger down.

5. Russell Cheyne

6. Adrian Murrell

7

8

1. Adrian Murrell

2. David Cannon

3. Allsport

1) The First Test between England and Australia during the 1989 Ashes Series. 2) A brightly coloured batsman skies a ball during the First Final of the World Series. The World Series was held annually in Australia throughout the decade and resulted in some exciting cricket, though many pruists bemoaned the abandonment of the traditional white clothing for team colours. 3) The West Indies bowler Roger Harper looses a fast ball against England. 4) Viv Richards of the West Indies sends a ball hurtling towards the boundary. The charismatic leader of the West Indies has been one of the foremost batsmen of the 1980s leading his test team to numerous successes and achieving some superb batting figures. At the one day match against England at Old Trafford in May 1984 he scored 189 not out in a matter of hours.

4. Adrian Murrell

3. Adrian Murrell

1. Adrian Murrell

2. Adrian Murrell

4. Adrian Murrell

5. Adrian Murrell

6. Adrian Murrell

1) Ian Botham takes a wicket during the Third Test against New Zealand in 1986. Botham is very probably the greatest all-round cricketer of the decade. By the end of the 1980s he had notched up 373 test wickets, over 100 catches and well over 5,000 test runs. He had begun the decade well in February 1980 in the Golden Jubilee Test Match against India when he took thirteen wickets and scored a century, becoming the first man ever to achieve such a double in a single test match. He continued to shine as a sportsman in the winter when he played soccer for a second division team. As the decade continued he became involved in various charity fund raising activities, including walking from John o'Groats to Landsend and later striding over the Alps with an elephant in emulation of Hannibal. 2) David Gower loses his wicket to a spectacular catch by Patterson of the West Indies. 3) Ian Botham hooks a bouncer towards the outfield. 4) The First Test between England and Australia in 1989. 5) Ian Botham bowling one of his effective medium paced balls. 6) Kapil Dev of India sends a ball for two.

1) Competitors in the 1987 Milk Race, otherwise known as the Tour de Britain. That year the gruelling race was won by Malcolm Elliot. The Milk Race was first held in 1951 when it was sponsored by the Daily Express as a conscious attempt to rival the Tour de France held annually across the Channel. The Milk Marketing Board took over sponsorship of the race, and changed its name, in 1958. The Milk Marketing Board, which controls all milk production in Britain has been a noticeable sports promoter during the 1980s, taking an interest in football as well as cycling. 2) Riders race around a corner during a town section of the 1987 Milk Race. 3) Laurent Fignon of France, in the headband, riding in the 1987 Paris-Nice race. Fignon won the race in 1983 and in 1984 when he beat 169 other competitors to the finishing post. 4) Paul Watson, his clothing covered with the names of his sponsors heads south in the Paris-Nice race of 1988. 5) Hair streaming in the wind, Gert-Jan Theunisse of the Netherlands races past a grain-field in the 17th or Briancon-Alpe d'Huez, stage of the 76th Tour de France in 1989. Facing page: Frank Weber of West Germany.

1. Roger Labrosse

2. Russell Cheyne

3. Jeff Allen

4. Graham Watson

5. Gerard Vandystadt

1. Oli Tennent

2. Agence Vandystadt

3. Agence Vandystadt

4. Gerard Vandystadt

1 & 2) Cyclo-cross is considered by many to be the most gruelling of all the cycling sports involving, as it does, not only high speed cycling but also cross-country running, hill climbing and strenuous struggles over obstacles. The sport makes heavy demands of machines as well as riders. The bicycles need to be tough enough to withstand the course yet light enough to be carried with ease. 3) Sean Kelly of Ireland leads the field in the 1989 Paris to Roubrix cyclo-cross. 4) The great French rider Martial Gayant races along a winter route. 5) The muddier side of cyclo-cross is shown here. It is up to the riders when to dismount as conditions become too hazardous for riding. 6) A competitor prepares to dismount as he approaches a particularly difficult hazard. 7) A tough cross-country section of cyclo-cross. 8) Beau Beat of Switzerland jogs through the mud with his bicycle slung over his shoulder. 9) Pascal Poisson of France in unusually clean condition at the start of a race. 10) Riders crest a hill on an off-road section. 11) Marc Madiot of France leads a group of competitors up a steep hill.

5. Pascal Rondeau

6. Patrick Vielcanet

7. Jean-Marc Loubat

8. Jean-Marc Loubat

10. Pascal Rondeau

9. Jean-Marc Barey

11. Yann Guichaoua

1. Bob Martin

2. Bob Martin

3. Mike Powell

4. Mike Powell

5. Pascal Rondeau

6. Simon Bruty

7. Simon Bruty

8. Mike Powell

9. Mike Powell

10. Mike Powell

11. Simon Miles

The sport of throwing darts originated in Ireland where they were used as a weapon, but the use of the modern board and darts was established in Lancashire in the late 19th century. 1) Eric Bristow who is possibly the greatest darts player of the 1980s. His record of titles includes five World Masters Championships, two World Cups and five World Professional Championships. He is seen here competing in the 1989 Embassy World Championships 2) Eric Bristow preparing to throw his third dart. 3) John Lowe Competing in the 1985 World Professional Darts Championship which he failed to win that year but gained victory in 1987. 4) Eric Bristow celebrates his triumph at the 1985 World Professional Championships. 5) Bob Anderson of England winning the World Professional Championship in 1988. 6) John Lowe at the 1986 Embassy World Championships. 7) Jocky Wilson of Scotland at the 1989 Embassy World Championship. 8) John Lowe on his way to winning the World Professional title in 1985. 9 & 10) Eric Bristow at the 1985 World Professional Championship. 11) Bobby George of England at the 1985 World Darts Championship.

1. Bob Martin

2. Bob Martin

3. Agence Vandystadt

The little-known sport of synchronised swimming made an entrance at the 1984 Los Angeles Olympics, much to the surprise of most sports fans around the world. Many people were not aware that the sport existed and it was, perhaps, rather too reminiscent of 1930s Hollywood musicals to be taken very seriously. However, the event became popular during the games, largely through the efforts of the American pair Tracy Ruiz and Candy Costee (4) who displayed a quite remarkable ability to co-ordinate their movements. The discipline and skill needed for the event were shown to be every bit as demanding as those required by figure skating, long accepted as a respectable sport. Ruiz and Costee defeated strong competition from Canada and elsewhere to clinch the Olympic title. 3) The Japanese entrants in the synchronised swimming duets.

4. Steve Powell

1. Pascal Rondeau

2. Pascal Rondeau

3. Pascal Rondeau

4. Pascal Rondeau

5. Jean-Marc Loubat

6. Tony Duffy

Diving is a perfectly natural way of entering water and has presumably been used since humans first swam. Its origins as a sport are rather obscure, but it was certainly established as a skill by the late 19th century and competitions were being held in the 1900s, by which time speed swimming had been a firmly established sport for over a century. Facing page 1) Mary Hummer of the United States at the 1987 Mission Bay event. Facing page 2) Henry Mathers at Mission Bay in 1987. 1) Daphne Jongjens of the Netherlands in pike position at the 1988 Seoul Olympics. 2) Daniel Bradshaw of the United States arches backward while competing in the springboard finals of the 1988 Seoul Olympics in which he was placed fifth. 3) The American Kelly McCormick bounces for height while competing in the springboard event at the Seoul Olympics. 4) Wendy Lucero in the springboard event at the Seoul Olympics. 5) The highboard. 6) The great Greg Louganis of the United States tumbling from the highboard at the 1984 Los Angeles Olympics. He won two gold medals at the games thus establishing himself as the foremost diver of the early 1980s. He had previously won three world championships and in 1986 went on to capture two more for the springboard and highboard events.

Fencing developed in the 16th and 17th centuries as an essential skill of courtly gentlemen who might, at any time, be called upon to defend their honour in a duel or to take up arms in warfare. Weapons were originally heavy and robust enough to cause serious wounds. Modern fencing, with its light weapons and lightning speed, did not appear until the 19th century. 1) Schmitt of West Germany parries a thrust from Riboud of France in the final combat of the epee event at the 1988 Seoul Olympics. Schmitt defeated Riboud to gain the gold medal, leaving the Frenchman with the silver. 2) West Germany's Schmitt loses a point to Chouvalov of the USSR at the Seoul Olympics, but he went on to win the epee bout. 3) Schmitt delivers a spectacular thrust to win the epee gold medal at the Seoul Olympics. 4) G. Scalzo of Italy brandishes his sabre over his head on his way to winning the bronze medal at the Seoul Olympics. 5) A member of the West German foil team reacts to the announcement that her team has won the gold at the Seoul Olympics. 6) Schmitt disarms Riboud during their final epee fight at the 1988 Seoul Olympics.

1. Jean-Marc Loubat

2. Jean-Marc Loubat

3. Pascal Rondeau

4. Russell Cheyne

5. Simon Bruty

6. Jean-Marc Loubat

1. Mike Powell

2. Mike Powell

3. Gray Mortimore

4. Joe Patronite

The modern combat sport of judo was developed during the last century in Japan. Its origins lie in the various systems of unarmed combat practised by the samurai, the warrior class of old Japan. When the samurai were stripped of power following the opening of Japan to the outside world, their combat skills were systemized into judo and taught to non-samurai at special schools. 1) Korean S. Kim struggles on despite injury against a French opponent in the under 86 kilogram event at the Seoul Olympics. 2) Osaka of Japan is thrown by Carmona of Brazil at the 1988 Seoul Olympics. 3) D. Stewart of Britain is dragged down by I Sosna in the under 95 kilogram event at the Seoul Olympics. 4) Garabett of France hurls his opponent Omaball to the ground in the 65 kilogram event at the Seoul Olympics. 5) The East German S. Loll struggles with Alexand of France. 6) A classic shoulder throw despatches a Norwegian at the Seoul Olympics.

5. Mike Powell

6. Gray Mortimore

1. Simon Bruty

2. Don Morley

3. David Cannon

4. David Cannon

5. Mike King

7. Ben Radford

6. David Cannon

8. David Cannon

The modern game of soccer developed from the old medieval sport of football during the 19th century as an attempt to make the tough sport safer and more regulated. England's Football Association was founded in 1863 and quickly standardised rules and regulations for the sport. 1) McLeish and Lineker struggle for possession of the ball during England's 1-0 victory over Scotland at Wembley in 1989 during the run up to the 1990 World Cup. 2) Kenny Dalglish of Liverpool holds the European Cup aloft after leading his team to victory in 1981. 3) Ruud Gullit of AC Milan intercepts a pass. 4) Diego Maradonna celebrates scoring a goal for Naples during his team's 3-2 defeat at the hands of AC Milan. Maradonna moved to Europe from his native Argentina after gaining fame in the 1982 World Cup. 5) Peter Shilton of England grabs the ball as it comes perilously close to his goal during England's match against Argentina in the 1986 World Cup. 6) A Dutch player leaps to head the ball in the English goal mouth during England's 3-1 defeat in the European Championships of 1989. 7) Peter Beardsly leaps to control a loose ball while playing for England in 1988. 8) Gary Lineker of England wins the ball from an opponent. 9) John Barnes of England robs the Polish player Prusik of the ball.

9. Ben Radford

Like many sports, soccer was originally strictly amateur with local men playing for village or works teams. As more and more fans attended matches, the clubs became able to pay star players to train full time, thus establishing professional soccer. Salaries and purchase prices for skilled players increased greatly as professional teams became more competitive and increasing amounts of money flowed through the game. Today players carry the names of sponsors on their shirts in order to gain extra money for their clubs. 1) Ratcliffe and Rosario leap for a high ball during Everton's 1-0 victory over Norwich. John Barnes of Liverpool and England runs with the ball. 3) Watson and Stein tussle for the ball during a match between Everton and Luton. 4) Kenny Dalglish of Liverpool lifts his arms to acknowledge the cheers of the crowd following a goal. Michael Thomas of Arsenal kicks the ball upfield to the forwards. 6) Gary Mabbut of Tottenham Hotspur stretches for a ball while Kerry Dixon of Chelsea prepares to be tackled during a match which ended in a 4-1 victory for Chelsea.

1. Simon Bruty

2. Simon Bruty

3. Simon Bruty

4. Trevor Jones

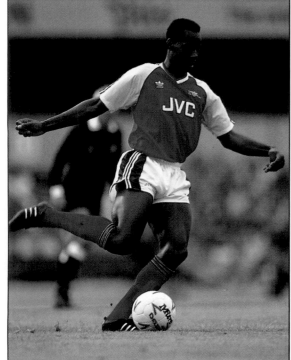

5. David Cannon

6. Roger Labrosse

1) Blue-shirted Sanchez powers the ball into the net, ensuring victory for Wimbledon in a 1-0 game against Liverpool. 2) Gary Lineker of Tottenham Hotspur, known as the Spurs, outdistances a Liverpool player as he races forward to take a shot at the opposition goal. 3) Ian Rush of Liverpool picks up a loose ball during a League Division One match against Norwich on 16th of September 1989, but to no avail for the match ended in a disappointing 0-0 draw. 4) Terry Butcher scores for Rangers in the Scottish Premier League. 5) Thousands of scarves, flowers and favours cover the goalmouth at Anfield, Liverpool's home ground, in the wake of the Hillsborough disaster of 1989, the tributes eventually covered half the pitch in a display of communal civic mourning. A cup tie match at Hillsborough had to be abandoned after nearly 100 people were crushed to death at the Liverpool supporters end. The exact causes of the tragedy were the subject of an official enquiry but a late surge of supporters arriving as the match began forced earlier arrivals against the crowd-control barriers from which there was no escape.

1. David Cannon

2. David Cannon

3. David Cannon

4. David Cannon

5. Pascal Rondeau

1) Diego Maradona of Argentina dives spectacularly to the ground in a goalmouth struggle during the 1986 World Cup competition. The somewhat theatrical behaviour of some South American players caused amusement among European spectators unused to such antics. It was suggested by a few disgruntled fans that the performances were intended to win sympathy from the referee. 2) Brian Robson of England turns with the ball. 3) Zoff and Gentile of Italy hold aloft the World Cup in triumph in 1982. 4) Scotland's McCleish leaps higher than Fashanu, Pearce or Walker to clear the ball from Scotland's goal-mouth following a corner during a fraught moment in the Rous Cup competition. The Rous Cup was held at Hampden Park in 1989 and ended in a 2-0 win for England over Scotland. 5) Peter Shilton performs one of his celebrated long kicks to push the ball upfield. Shilton is arguably the finest English goal keeper since Gordon Banks played in the 1960s. 6) Jacobs and Schumacher of West Germany successfully struggle for the ball in their own goalmouth.

1. Gerard Vandystadt

2. Simon Bruty

3. Steve Powell

4. David Cannon

5. Mike King

6. David Cannon

The World Cup is the most prestigious competition in soccer. It was first held in 1930 and is now held two years after each Olympic Games. For many months before each competition international teams play qualifying matches to determine which national teams will take part in the actual play-offs. These culminate in a final match televised world-wide where the cup is won. The original gold cup was won outright by Brazil in 1970 and replaced by the present trophy, which is not actually a cup but a statuette, for the 1974 final. 1) Rummenigge drives the ball past defender and goalkeeper to score during Argentina's spectacular and entertaining 3-2 defeat of West Germany. 2) Jakobs of West Germany performs an overhead kick to rob Argentina's Valdano of the ball during the European teams 3-2 defeat. 3) Gullit and Voller involved in a tangle of limbs as they try to gain control of a loose ball during Holland's 2-1 win over West Germany. 4) Platini of France holds his arms aloft in triumph after scoring one of his team's five goals against Brazil, which managed to score four goals in the same match. 5) Gary Lineker of England prepares to leap for a high ball in competition with two Polish players in a match which England won 3-0.

1. David Cannon

2. David Cannon

3. David Cannon

4. David Cannon

5. Mike King

1. David Cannon

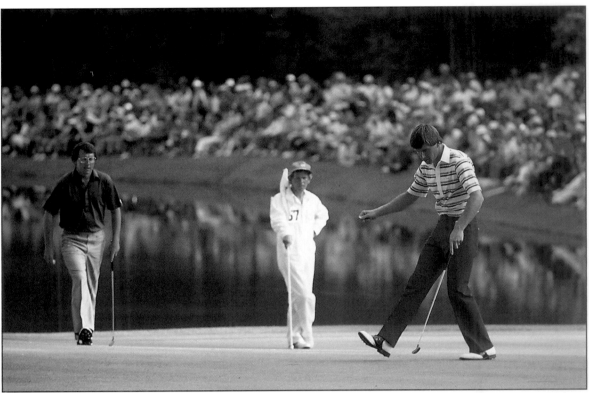

2. David Cannon

The game of golf appears to be of Scottish origin, although some other nations contest this theory with claims of their own. The antiquity of the game in Scotland is, however, beyond doubt. It was first mentioned in 1457 while a folk-song bemoaning the murder of the Earl of Moray in 1592 described him as 'a broad gallant who played at the ball'. The three oldest golf clubs in the world are all Scottish. The Royal and Ancient Club of St Andrew's was founded in 1754, the Honourable company of Edinburgh Golfers in 1744 and the Royal Burgess Golfing Society in 1735, though reliable records for the last club are rather patchy. 1) Sandy Lyle lining up a putt during the 1988 U.S. Masters. 2) Nick Faldo pacing the green during the 1984 U.S. Masters. 3) The colourful backdrop supplied by flowers bordering the fairway at the 1989 U.S. Masters. 4) Sandy Lyle raises his club aloft to celebrate the winning putt of the 1988 U.S. Masters. 5) Seve Ballesteros drives the ball during the 1988 U.S. Masters.

3. David Cannon

4. David Cannon

5. David Cannon

Originally golf clubs were made of wood. Great skill was required in choosing shafts of sufficient strength and sturdiness to allow the player to control the flight of his ball properly. The introduction of steel golf clubs in the 1920s allowed for a much greater range of club heads as well as for stronger shafts. Players were thus able to drive balls further and more accurately than ever before, and because of using these clubs altered the accepted pars for their courses. 1) Greg Norman of Australia clears his ball from a bunker at Royal Troon during the British Open of 1989. 2) The American golfer Curtis Strange ponders the best method of making a long putt during the 1988 U.S. Open. 3) Ian Woosnam of Great Britain lifts his ball from a bunker during the 1988 match between teams from Britain and Australia which was referred to as the Golfing Ashes in imitation of the cricketing Ashes contested between the two nations. 4) The 1988 U.S. Open was won by Sandy Lyle. 5) Craig Stadler scoops his ball out of a bunker during the 1988 U.S. Masters.

1. Simon Bruty

2. Simon Bruty

3. Dan Smith

4. Simon Bruty

5. David Cannon

1. Jean-Marc Loubat

2. David Cannon

1) Seve Ballesteros peers anxiously from the trees to watch the progress of a ball which he has hit when only able to see part of the green at which he was aiming. 2) Seve Ballesteros cradles the silver trophy he gained for winning the British Open at St Andrew's in Scotland in 1984. 3) Sandy Lyle strolls away from a hole with the ball lifted to acknowledge the applause of the crowd for a fine birdy which he achieved on his way to win the 1985 British Open. 4) Greg Norman of Australia watches a putt sink home in front of a crowd of spectators well protected against the rain which marred much of the 1989 U.S. Masters. 5) Tom Watson lifts his ball from a bunker, or trap, during the 1988 U.S. Masters at Augusta in Georgia. 6) Tom Watson kisses the elegant silver jug which is presented to the winner of the British Open in 1982. Though he won the trophy he failed to beat his own record of 72 holes in 268 strokes which he achieved in the 1977 British Open. 7) The Australian player Greg Norman squints into the sun as he anxiously watches the progress of a drive during the 1989 Australian Open. 8) The West German player Bernhard Langer is helped out of a deep bunker during the 1987 Ryder Cup which the European team won. The Ryder Cup was founded in 1927 as a competition between the United States and Britain. By 1977 the Americans had achieved such a dominance in the Ryder Cup that the competition was reorganised so that a European team replaced the British. The result was that in 1985 a European team lead by the British player Tony Jacklin (10) took the title from the Americans for the first time in 30 years. 12) Two years later the Europeans repeated their success in the Ryder Cup, which is held every alternate year, when they were again led by Tony Jacklin. 9) Seve Ballesteros punches the air after sinking the putt which won him the 1984 British Open. 11) Mark Calcavecchia celebrates the presentation of the cherished trophy for the British Open in 1989 at Royal Troon in front of the press.

3. David Cannon

4. David Cannon

5. David Cannon

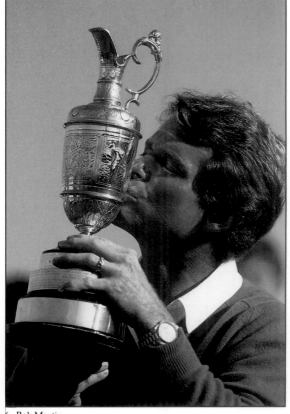

6. Bob Martin

7. Pascal Rondeau

8. David Cannon

9. David Cannon

10. David Cannon

11. David Cannon

12. Simon Bruty

1. David Cannon

2. Simon Bruty

3. David Cannon

4. David Cannon

The much esteemed U.S. Masters championship was first held in 1934 at the Augusta National Golf Course at the charming Georgian town of Augusta. The course (1 & 3) is one of the most attractive in the world with fairways threading their way between woods and greens backed by placid bodies of water, all of which form additional hazards for the golfers. 2) Curtis Strange scoops his ball from a bunker during the 1988 U.S. Open in a superb shot which won him the hole. Strange achieved a remarkable feat in the 1987 season when he managed to win nearly $926,000 in prize money, more than any other player, but without gaining a single major title. This success was due to sustained form which brought him a string of high placings in nearly every competition he entered. 4) Nick Faldo scatters sand in the wind as he pushes his ball on to the green during the 1988 U.S. Masters. 5) Play at the Belfry under a blazing sun during the 1985 Ryder Cup which was lost by the United States team for the first time in decades.

5. Bob Martin

1) Balmy summer weather brought out large crowds to watch the 1988 U.S. Masters at Augusta, Georgia. The spectators were not disappointed by the standard of play which was consistently high and culminated in a well-deserved win for Sandy Lyle. 2) The beautiful club house of the Royal and Ancient Club of St Andrews seen across the green of the 18th hole. The club dates back to 1754, just nine years after the clansmen of Bonnie Prince Charlie marched south in their doomed attempt to defeat the troops loyal to King George II. 3) Tom Kite pitches his ball on to the green during the 1989 U.S. Masters. 4) The British player Nick Faldo who won the U.S. Masters competition in 1989. 5) The 16th Cypress Point hole at the Pebble Beach Golf Course, arguably the most difficult in the world. It involves driving the ball along precipitous cliffs and across extremely broken ground. Particularly adventurous golfers may attempt to reach the green by driving across the sea, but risk losing balls to the waves.

1. David Cannon

2. David Cannon

3. David Cannon

4. David Cannon

5. David Cannon

1) Hundreds of spectators line the fairway beneath a warm Georgian sun during the 1988 U.S. Open. 2) Bernhard Langer shoots into the wind from a bunker during the 1988 U.S. Open and is rewarded by a shower of fine white sand blown back on him. 3) Stadler drops a shot during the 1988 U.S. Masters when his ball fails to clear the bunker and rolls back almost to his feet. 4) The Spanish player Olazabal brings his club down in a sweeping stroke to drive his ball along the fairway during his unsuccessful bid for the 1989 U.S. Masters. 5) A determined Jack Nicklaus lifts his ball from a deep bunker during the 1986 U.S. Masters. Nicklaus is considered by many to be the most successful player ever with over 20 major international titles to his name, including a record 4 wins in the U.S. Open. 6) Bernhard Langer drives off along the beautifully tended fairway of the Augusta National Golf Course during the 1988 U.S. Masters. A gigantic horseshoe of thousands of spectators stands in the sun to watch the final putting on a vital hole in the 1988 U.S. Masters.

1. David Cannon

2. David Cannon

3. David Cannon

4. David Cannon

5. David Cannon

6

7

1. Pascal Rondeau

2. Bernard Asset

Motor racing began almost as soon as the motor car was invented with proud new owners eager to put their modern contraptions through the speed paces to which they were accustomed to subjecting their horses. These early races were held on open roads, but the danger of this was soon appreciated and the first motor racing track was laid out in 1896. Modern Grand Prix racing is between highly specialised machines rather than the road vehicles used in early races. 1) The cars race away from the grid at the start of the Portuguese Grand Prix in 1989, filling the air with hot exhaust fumes. 2) The bright red Ferrari driven by Berger during the 1989 French Grand Prix. Ferrari have won the manufacturers' world title more times than any other company. 3) Alain Prost races his Mclaren to victory in the 1988 Brazilian Grand Prix. 5) Nigel Mansel pushes his Lotus through the rain in the 1989 Italian Grand Prix, throwing up a cloud of spray. 4) Ayrton Senna powers his Ferrari to his first Grand Prix victory in Portugal in 1985. 6) The Italian driver de Cesaris driving through the drizzle on his way to capture 3rd place in the Canadian Grand Prix of 1989. 7) A thick cloud of spray covers the trailing cars during the early stages of the 1989 Belgian Grand Prix at Spa. The start had been delayed because of heavy rain.

6

3. Simon Bruty

4. Pascal Rondeau

5. Bernard Asset

7

1. Pascal Rondeau

6

2. Jean-Marc Loubat

1) British driver Nigel Mansell driving his Ferrari in the tightly contested 1989 German Grand Prix at which he achieved third place. 2) Alain Prost leads the field in his Mclaren in 1987. Prost was without doubt the most successful Grand Prix driver of the decade with over 30 victories to his name, 7 of which were won in 1984 alone. 3) The brightly coloured car driven by Allesandro Nannini of Italy who achieved 4th place in the 1989 Portuguese Grand Prix. 4) Pier Luigi Martini driving his vehicle to 5th place in the 1989 Portuguese Grand Prix. 5) Sparks fly from beneath the Ferrari driven by Gerhard Berger as the metal strikes the ground in the 1989 Belgian Grand Prix which Berger failed to finish. 6) Nigel Mansell racing to victory in his Ferrari at the 1989 Hungarian Grand Prix. Easily the most promising British driver to emerge in the 1980s, Mansell came close to achieving some brilliant wins but never quite managed to emulate the success of Jim Clark or Stirling Moss of earlier generations. 7) Ayrton Senna of Brazil powering out of a corner during the 1989 Portuguese Grand Prix.

3. Pascal Rondeau

4. Pascal Rondeau

5. Pascal Rondeau

7

7) During the 1989 French Grand Prix the opening lap was brought to a sudden and spectacular end when Maurico Gugelmin of Brazil was involved in a violent crash in which his car was almost completely destroyed. Marshals rushed to the scene with fire extinguishers while Gugelmin struggled to escape from the wreckage (1). Seemingly miraculously Gugelmin was uninjured. He later climbed into the reserve car and set the fastest race lap. 2) The Italian de Cesaris ploughs down a grassy bank during the 1985 Austrian Grand Prix, ending his chances of victory. 3) The vehicles of Patrese and Nelson Piquet became involved in a crash and ball of flames at the 1985 Monaco Grand Prix from which both men escaped without serious injury. 4) Marshals struggle to free the badly injured Didier Pironi of France from his wrecked Ferrari which crashed during practice laps in the 1982 Grand Prix at Hockenheim. 5) Daly and Tyrrell collide during the 1981 Monaco Grand Prix. 6) The second start of the 1987 Austrian Grand Prix came to an end in a multiple pile-up.

1. Pascal Rondeau

2. Patrick Behar

3. Bernard Asset

4. Agence Vandystadt

6

5. Bernard Asset

7

The Grand Prix circuit has developed slowly since the the 'great prize' was offered nearly a century ago and now includes many races. 1) Gerhard Berger settles into his car for the 1988 Brazilian Grand Prix. 2) Flames leap from the rear of the Minardi vehicle during the 1986 Italian Grand Prix moments before the driver withdrew from the race. 3) The wet-weather tyres of Thierry Boutsen's Williams car throw up fine spray as he zips through a chicane during the 1989 Belgian Grand Prix. 4) A dramatic aerial view of the collision between Nelson Piquet and Patrese which occurred during the 1985 Monaco Grand Prix. 5) The first start of the 1989 San Marino Grand Prix which proved abortive. The San Marino Grand Prix is a major factor in the economy of the tiny city state of San Marino, an anachronistic hangover from the Italian renaissance. 6) Nigel Mansell flies past brightly coloured trackside decor in 1987. 7) The young British driver Johnny Herbert racing at Brands Hatch in the Formula 3000 in 1988 at which time he was looked upon as the rising British star in the racing world. 8) Nigel Mansell receives last minute advice from the pit staff before taking up his position on the grid in his Ferrari for the 1989 French Grand Prix. 9) Emmanuele Pirro of Italy awaits the start of the 1989 French Grand Prix with a helmet advertising a clothing manufacturer from his home nation.

1. Simon Bruty

2. Bernard Asset

3. Alain Patrice

4. Patrick Behar

5. Bernard Asset

6. Jean-Marc Loubat

7. Pascal Rondeau

8. Jean-Marc Loubat

9. Pascal Rondeau

Facing page: Anton Senna raises his hand as flames leap from the rear of his Lotus vehicle as oil catches fire during the 1986 Grand Prix at Rio de Janeiro's Jacarepagua Circuit.
1) Sparks fly as the undersides of vehicles heavily laden with fuel touch the ground at the start of the 1989 Brazilian Grand Prix. Seconds later Anton Senna and Gerhard Berger clipped each others cars and crashed. 2) Brian Henton-Toleman climbs from the mangled wheel-less wreckage of what was once a racing car during the 1981 British Grand Prix. 3) An apparently anxious glance from Alain Prost as he adjusts his driving gloves seconds before beginning driving in the 1989 Italian Grand Prix. This was his first outing after the accident at the San Marino Grand Prix which forced him out of the race. 4) Pit staff make adjustments within the cockpit of Gerhard Berger's vehicle before wheeling it out on to the grid for the start of the 1989 Brazilian Grand Prix. 5) Eddie Irvine clips a corner in a Formula 3000 race at Brands Hatch in 1989 causing his wheels to lift from the ground, though he quickly regained control.

1. Pascal Rondeau

2. Emmanuel Zurini

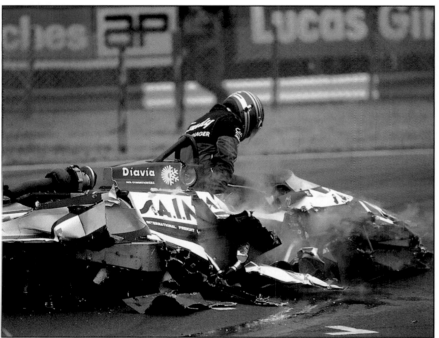

3. Pascal Rondeau

4. Pascal Rondeau

5. Pascal Rondeau

1. Bob Martin

2. Bob Martin

3. Christian Petit

4. Russell Cheyne

5. Bob Martin

1. Gray Mortimore

Greyhounds were originally bred as sight hounds, dogs trained to hunt small game by sight. They were used to run down hares in short, rapid chases which the quarry rarely escaped. In some areas the dogs are still used for hare-coursing, when they chase live hares along a course, but it is now more usual for them to chase mechanical hares around a track. 1) Greyhounds spring from the traps at the Hollywood track where the dogs (2) are also racing. 3) French greyhounds racing on a dirt track by floodlight. 4) An Australian race run with special plastic muzzles little used outside greyhound racing. 5) Racing at the Hollywood track. 6) Dogs rounding a corner at the Hackney track in London. 7) The runaway winner of a race held on 18th May 1989 at the Hackney track. 8) A close race at Hackney in May 1989. 9) A study of the unbeaten world champion greyhound Ballyreagan Bob which won an amazing 32 consecutive races in the mid-1980s. 10) Backmarkers in a race at the Hollywood track.

2. Gray Mortimore

3. Gray Mortimore

4. Simon Bruty

5. Bob Martin

1. Yann Guichaoua

2. Bob Martin

3. Pascal Rondeau

4. Gray Mortimore

5. Yann Guichaoua

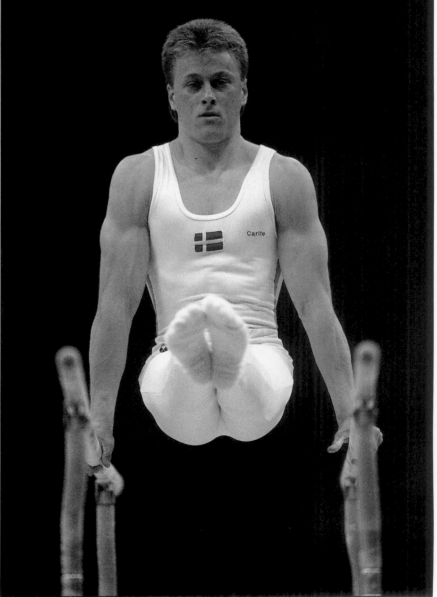

6. Pascal Rondeau

1) Sylvio Kroll in his silver medal winning performance on the parallel bars at the 1988 Seoul Olympics. 2 & 5) Dmitri Bilozerchev of the USSR performing on the horizontal bar in the 1988 Seoul Olympics where he won the bronze in addition to a silver medal for the rings and a bronze medal for all round gymnastics. 3) Dominick Minicucci of the United States springing into action for the compulsory exercise on the horse at the Seoul Olympics. 4) Ulf Hoffman of the East German male gymnastics team spins on the rings at the Seoul Olympics. 6) Johan Jonasson of Swede begins his routine at the Seoul Olympics. 7) Sven Tippelt prepares to lift himself on to the parallel bars in order to start his demanding routine. 8) Terry Bartlett of Great Britain in action on the vaulting horse during the team event at the Seoul Olympics. 9) Conner, Vidmar and Grosfield lift their arms in triumph as they receive the gold medals for team gymnastics at the 1984 Los Angeles Olympic Games. 10) Valeri Lioukine of the USSR lines up for a scissor swing at the Seoul Olympics. 11) Vladimir Artemov of the USSR, recognised as possibly the leading male gymnast of the decade after picking up the gold medal for all round gymnastics, the gold medal for parallel bars, the gold medal for horizontal bars and the silver medal for floor exercises at the Seoul Olympics.

7. Bob Martin

8. Pascal Rondeau

9. Steve Powell

10. Pascal Rondeau

11. Bob Martin

1. Bob Martin

2. Bob Martin

3. Roger Labrosse

The modern disciplines of gymnastics date back to a system of physical exercises developed in Germany late last century. 1) Marina Lobach of the USSR performing her winning routine of rhythmic gymnastics at the Seoul Olympics. 2) Eugenia Golea of Romania performing in the women's team gymnastics final at the Seoul Olympics. 3) Marina Lobach of the USSR performing in Russia in 1989. 4) Julianne McNamara of the USA somersaults on the beam in a routine which helped her maintain her leading role in women's gymnastics for much of the decade. 5) Elena Chouchounova of the USSR balances on the beam in the women's team gymnastics final at the Seoul Olympics. Chouchounova won the gold in the all round gymnastics event.

4. Steve Powell

5. Bob Martin

1) Natalia Lachtchenova of the USSR leaps as part of her spectacular beam routine in the women's gymnastics team final at the Seoul Olympics. 2 & 4) The popular and immensely successful Julianne McNamara of the United States performing a backward somersault on the beam while dressed in a costume aptly decorated with stars and stripes. 3) The talented Eugenia Golea of Romania slowly lifts her legs over her head as she hand stands while performing the compulsory exercises on the beam during the team event at the Seoul Olympics in 1988. 5) Romi Kessler of Switzerland springs before performing a complex series of turns and handsprings in the floor exercises event.

1. David Cannon

2. Gray Mortimore

3. Mike Powell

4. Simon Bruty

Hockey is one of the oldest games in the world. It can be traced directly to the 13th century while similar games were being played 3,000 years ago. 1) Ian Taylor of Great Britain dives to save a goal at the 1988 Seoul Olympics. 2) Sean Kelly of Great Britain beats Korean opponents to the ball in a match at the Seoul Olympics which ended in a 2-2 draw. 3) An Indian player at full stretch is beaten by West Germany at the Seoul Olympics. 4) The Australian defence during the World Hockey Championships of 1986. 5) P. Kerly and Colin Batch struggle for the ball during a match between Australia and England during the 1986 Hockey World Cup. 6) A determined race for a loose ball during the match between Australia and Argentina at the Seoul Olympics. 7) The Polish team captain Abgieniew Rachwalski races with the ball during a World Cup match with West Germany. A Spanish player tumbles to the ground as team mate Ignacio Escude scoops the ball from a Pakistan player at the Seoul Olympics. The Spanish effort failed for Pakistan won 5-1. 9) Australia plays England in the 1986 World Cup. 10) Hockey World Cup 1986. 11) V. Kumnar of India beats J. Shaw of England to the ball in a World Cup match.

5. Adrian Murrell

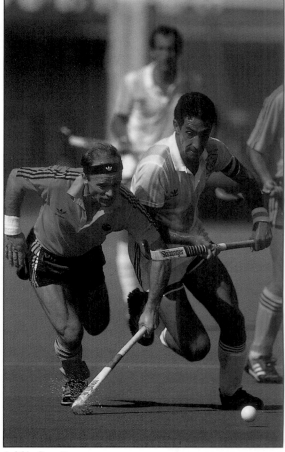

6. Mike Powell

7. Simon Bruty

8. Gray Mortimore

9 Simon Bruty

10. Bob Martin

11. Simon Bruty

Exactly when horses were first ridden by humans is unclear, but would seem to have been some time around 3,000 BC when nomads on the Eurasian steppes learnt how to tame the wild horse as well as to hunt it. Horsemanship rapidly became important not only for transport but also in hunting, herding and warfare. Competitions in riding skills were undoubtedly held at an early period, though the first written reference to horse racing over fixed distances comes from ancient Greece when the event was added to the Olympic Games in the 7th century BC. Since that time the sport has taken a variety of forms and changes. The medieval war horse needed to have great stamina and to be well behaved in the noise of battle rather than to be speedy. Only with the demise of the armoured knight did speed become once again essential to horsemen. 1) The strong field rounds a corner during the 1987 Ever Ready Epsom Derby, a race which was won by Reference Point (6). 2) Don't Forget Me racing for the line to win narrowly in the 1987 2,000 Guineas. 3) The field turning Tattenham Corner during the 1988 Ever Ready Epsom Derby. 4) Royal Ascot, June 1988. 5) A race starts from the stalls at Sandown in 1987. 7) High Tech Girl, ridden by Graham Starkey, racing to victory in the 1984 Queen Mary Stakes at Ascot.

1. David Cannon

2. Chris Cole

3. Gray Mortimore

4. Trevor Jones

5. Joe Patronite

The most important and prestigious steeplechase race in the world is the Grand National which was first run in 1847 at Liverpool's Aintree race course over 30 fences. Except for interruption during the World Wars, the race has been held ever year since over the same course. The immense size of the fences has recently caused concern among safety experts and the heights have been reduced. However, jockeys tend to take the smaller jumps at greater speed and accidents still occur. 1) Brown Trix falls and is killed at the infamous Beechers Brook during the 1989 Grand National. 2) Horses clearing the ditch on the landing side of Beechers Brook during the 1989 Grand National. 3) The grey Dark Ivy rolls on the ground after a fatal fall at Beechers Brook during the 1987 Grand National. 4) Steeplechasing at Wincanton. 5) Racing on the ice at St Moritz in Switzerland during the winter of 1989. The frozen lakes of Alpine resorts make ideal, if temporary racecourses where the horsing fraternity can indulge their taste even when on skiing holidays.

1. Bob Martin

2. Bob Martin

3. Bob Martin

4. Trevor Jones

5. Bob Martin

1. Dan Smith

2. Chris Cole

3. Mike Powell

4. Trevor Jones

1) The final stages of the 1989 Prix de l'Arc de Triomphe, the premier horse race of France. The race was first instituted in 1920 as a direct rival to the classics being run in Britain and has since established itself as one of the most important flat races in Europe. 2) Trempolino streaks across the finishing line to win the 1987 Prix de l'Arc de Triomphe in the fastest time to date at 2 minutes 26 seconds. 3) Horses race for the line at the 1988 Kentucky Derby, which was first run on the Churchill Downs in 1875 as a New World rival to the Epsom Derby. Kentucky is the heart of the American race horse industry with a number of stables and studs feeding their charges on the rich blue-green grass of the state. 4) The short-stirrup and crouched posture of the modern jockey first developed in America.

1) A competitor on the skeleton sled races downhill at St Moritz. The skeleton sled was invented at St Moritz for use on the famous Cresta Run which was constructed in 1884 and where speeds of over 80 kilometres (50 miles) per hour are regularly obtained. 2) Eric Heiden of the United States who won five gold medals at the 1980 Winter Olympic Games. 3) Dan Jansen of the United States photographed at the 1987 World Cup speed skating championships. 4) The Russian two-man luge team of Melnik and Alexeev speed past at the 1988 Calgary Winter Olympic Games. The chief difference between luge and sled is that in luge the rider travels feet first rather than head first down the course. 5) Bonnie Blair, champion woman skater of the United States, photographed in 1987.

2. Don Morley

1. Yann Guichaoua

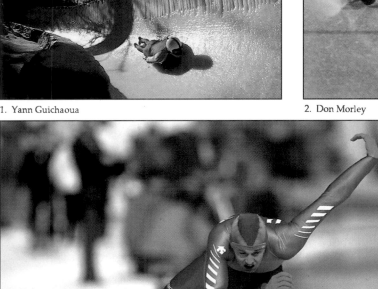
3. Gerard Vandystadt

4. Gerard Vandystadt

5. Bob Martin

1. Mike Powell

The origins of ice hockey are obscure but are most likely to have been in northern Europe during the late middle ages. During the 20th century the game spread rapidly across the world and is now played in many countries. 1) Wayne Gretsky of the Oilers anxiously awaits his turn on the ice during a match with the Kings in 1987. 2) The gold-medal winning United States team at the 1980 Lake Placid Winter Olympic Games. 3) Two American players celebrate victory over Finland during the 1980 Winter Olympic Games. 4) The puck rips past the keeper during a women's ice hockey match. 5) The Swiss ice hockey team discuss tactics at their goal before skating out to be beaten 8-4 by the United States team. 6) Luc Robitaille of the Kings skating with the puck during a 1987 match against the Oilers.

3. Steve Powell

2. Steve Powell

4. Bob Martin

5. Gray Mortimore

6. Mike Powell

The modern winter sport of figure skating and ice dancing was brought to near perfection by the British pair Jayne Torvill and Christopher Dean during the early 1980s when they took a string of titles with maximum marks, including the gold at the 1984 Winter Olympics in Sarajevo. 1, 3, 4, 5, 7 & 9) Torvill and Dean performing in their 1985 World Tour which they took to numerous countries and played to sell-out audiences. The tour included not only their famous routines but also a number of spectacular dance numbers by a skating troupe and some magnificent costumes. 2) Torvill and Dean skate in unaccustomed formal wear when they appeared with the Russian Allstars in Los Angeles in 1990. 6) Torvill and Dean skate in graceful blue outfits. 8) Torvill and Dean strike a dramatic pose while taking part in the 1986 Sports Aid Gala to raise money for charities. 10) Torvill and Dean perform their famous 'bolero routine' at Obertsdorf in Germany in January 1984. 11) Torvill and Dean acknowledging the applause of the audience after completing their routine.

1. Bob Martin

2. Mike Powell

3. Bob Martin

4. Bob Martin

5. Bob Martin

6. Trevor Jones

7. Bob Martin

8. Bob Martin

9. Bob Martin

10 Bob Martin

11. Dave Cannon

1. Caryn Levy

2. Robert Beck

3. Caryn Levy

The most important motor race in the New World is the Indianapolis 500 which takes its name from the town where it is held and the fact that drivers must cover 500 miles of track. The race was first held in 1911 and has continued to be raced every May ever since. Endurance of machine over long distances such as this are as important as driving skills. 1) Screeching out of the pits after a fast tyre change. 2) Rick Mears celebrates his victory in the 1988 race for which he was rewarded with $800,000. 3) Danny Sullivan's vehicle just prior to the 1987 race. 4) Al Unser racing to victory in 1987. 5) The pit crew swarm around Rick Mears during the 1988 race which he went on to win. 6) A lightning wheel change during the 1987 race.

4. Caryn Levy

1. Pascal Rondeau

2. Yann Guichaoua

3. Pascal Rondeau

4. Gerard Vandystadt

First held in 1923 the Le Man 24 Hour Race is recognised as the greatest endurance test for racing cars and their drivers. 1) In 1989 the British Jaguar team failed to repeat their success in the Le Mans 24 Hour Race of the previous year. 2) The Hobbs-Konrad team race in the 1988 Le Mans 24 Hour Race in a Porsche 962C. 3) The Mercedes of Schlesser and Baldi at the Brands Hatch 1000. 4) Jan Lammers and Johnny Dumfries driving their Jaguar XJR 9 to a stunning victory in the 1988 Le Mans 24 hour race, the first Jaguar victory for 31 years. In winning the team set a new record by completing 5332 kilometres (3,313 miles) in the race. 5) Winter and Jelinski driving their Porsche 962C in the 1988 Le Mans 24 Hour Race. 6) The Mercedes competitor in the 1989 Le Mans 24 Hour Race. 7) Brundle and Nielsen driving their Jaguar XJR 9 in the 1988 Le Mans 24 hour. 8) The Porsche pit team work frantically to change tyres during the 1988 Le Mans 24 Hour Race. 9) Kennedy and Dieudonne racing in the 1989 Le Mans 24 Hour Race. 10) Wolleck and Stuck drive through the night on their way to 3rd place in the 1989 Le Mans.

5. Yann Guichaoua

6. Pascal Rondeau

7. Yann Guichaoua

8. Pascal Rondeau

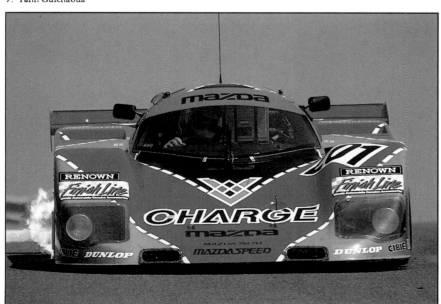

9. Pascal Rondeau

10. Pascal Rondeau

The idea of putting an internal combustion engine on to a robust bicycle was put into practice as soon as engines light enough were invented. By the close of the last century the first organised races on specially built tracks were being run, though special racing machines were not developed until well into this century. Modern racing bikes can develop and maintain extremely high speeds on the track. 1) Riders almost scrape the ground as they round a corner during the 1987 Trans-Atlantic competition between the United States and Britain at Brands Hatch. 2) The 1988 Bol d'Or. 3) The Kawasaki GPX team at the 24 Heur du Mans Race. 4) Kenny Roberts of the United States speeding round a corner in the 1984 Trans-Atlantic competition. 5) The British rider Bob McElnea competing in the 1988 Dutch Grand Prix on a Suzuki RGV500. 6) The 1988 Bol d'Or. 7) The British rider Wayne Gardener taking part in the 1984 Trans-Atlantic competition. 8) Cutting a corner perilously close during the 1987 Trans-Atlantic competition.

1. Chris Cole

2. Oli Tennent

3 Pascal Rondeau

4. Bob Martin

5. Yann Guichaoua

6. Oli Tennent

7

8

1. Simon Bruty

2. Pascal Rondeau

3. Joe Patronite

1) Chili Pierfrancesco powers through a corner during the 1988 British Grand Prix. 2) J.L. Battistini on the Honda No.1 machine during the 24 Heurs du Mans race. 3) The distinctively blue clad C. Sarron of France riding his Gauloise Blondes Yamaha 500cc in the 1989 French Grand Prix. 4) The American rider Wayne Rainey racing to 3rd place in the 1989 British Grand Prix. 5) Eddie Lawson of the United States lifts the front wheel of his Yamaha during the 1987 British Grand Prix. 6) Kevin Schwantz of the United States exuberantly wheelies his Suzuki machine and raised a clenched fist to celebrate his victory in the 1989 British Grand Prix. 7) The American rider Eddie Lawson racing his Honda to take second place in the 1989 British Grand Prix. Lawson is possibly the greatest rider of the decade, taking the World Championship in three successive years, 1984, 1985 and 1986. 8) Wayne Rainey speeding down the straight on his Yamaha on his way to winning the 1988 Grand Prix.

4. Pascal Rondeau

5. Simon Bruty

6. Pascal Rondeau

7. Pascal Rondeau

8. Simon Bruty

1) Christan Sarron of France tumbles from his Yamaha and slides along the track during the 1988 British Motorcycle Grand Prix, managing to escape without serious injury. 2) Nail MacKenzie lifts the front wheel of his Honda from the ground during the 1987 British Motorcycle Grand Prix. 3) The French rider Raymond Roche takes a corner during the 1988 British Motorcycle Grand Prix. 4) Lavado on a brightly coloured Yamaha 500 speeds round a corner during the 1986 French Motorcycle Grand Prix. 5) The heavily sponsored Eddie Lawson wearing the bright colour of the sponsor on his leathers, helmet and bike as he speeds round a corner. 6) Kevin Schwarez takes part in the 1988 British Motorcycle Grand Prix while carrying the logo of his sponsor on his leathers and bike. Commercial sponsorship plays a major role in modern motor sports as only in this way can riders and teams meet the soaring costs of up-to-date machinery and technology.

1. Simon Bruty

2. Simon Bruty

3. Simon Bruty

5

4. Alain Patrice

6

1. DonMorley

3. Simon Bruty

4. Mike Powell

2. Don Morley

5. Alain Marty

6. Simon Miles

Perhaps the most thrilling and exciting motorcycle sport is motocross in which riders negotiate hazards and obstacles as they power cross country on dirt tracks and worn paths. 1) Drivers surge around the first corner of a Motocross race. 2) Andre Malherre leads the field in a spectacular leap at the top of a steep rise before a large audience. 3) Eric Geboers throws his bike in a large leap while powering through a wooded section of the Belgian 500 Motocross Grand Prix in which he eventually finished in second place. 4) Pierre Lassut of Belgium thrusts out his leg to steady himself from sliding on mud while speeding through driving rain in the Belgian 500 Motocross Grand Prix. 5) Bruno Auquier of France loses control of his machine in a sandpit during a French Motocross championship. 6) Determined riders hunch over their machines as they await the start signal for the Belgian 500 Motocross Grand Prix. 7) The heel of Eric Geboers kicks up a spurt of dirt as his corners his bike during the Belgian 500 Motocross Grand Prix in which he attained second place. 8) Hakan Carlqvist of Sweden speeding through a shower of mud thrown up by a previous rider during the Belgian 500 Motocross Grand Prix. 9) Georges Jobe speeds past spectators on his way to win the Belgian 500 Motocross Grand Prix. 10) Dust flies as a rider pushes his machine through a pit of dry dirt. 11) Riders drive through flying mud in a French motocross event.

7. Simon Bruty

8. Mike Powell

9. Simon Bruty

10. J.P. Lenfant

11. Pat Boulland

1. Chris Cole

2. Alain Patrice

1) Specially prepared bikes take to the snow in the 1987 World Ice-Speedway Championships. The bikes are fitted with tyres from which project needle sharp spikes of steel designed to spear the ice and give a secure hold. 2) A. Klatowski of the USSR tumbles to the ice in a shower of snow beside the Finnish rider Peter Nybo during the Motorcylce Ice Race Championships of 1988. 3) The French team of Herve and Luc corner through the mud during the sidecar motocross event. 4) Sidecar passengers stand ready to lean their weight as required on corners during the 1988 Sidecar Motocross Grand Prix. 5) Athletic sidecar passengers scamper around their lightweight coachwork in an attempt to give extra stability to the machine during the 1988 Sidecar Motocross Grand Prix. 6) Team-mates leap in unison during the 1987 Molson Supercross Championships which is raced on a specially constructed course under cover from the elements. 7) An exuberant display during the 1987 Molson Supercross Championships. 8) A fine leap during the 1984 Supercross Championships. 9) The mass start of the 250cc San Diego Supercross.

3. Gerard Vandystadt

4. Oli Tennent

5. Oli Tennent

6. Gray Mortimore

7. Gray Mortimore

8. Pat Behar

9. Mike Powell

3. Oli Tennent

The glamorous sport of powerboat racing dates back to 1903 when the first trophy was presented. 1) A 4-man powerboat crashes through the seas during the 1988 World Powerboat Championships. 2) The Italian boat crewed by Cavaliere, Ballarin and Palchetti speeds across a calm Mediterranean off the fashionable French resort of St Tropez during the 1988 Powerboat Grand Prix. 3) The Italian *Babycresci* boat surges across a glittering sea during the Guernsey Championships of 1987. 4) The Italian *Babycresci* boat crewed by Ballabio, Morosini and Toriani leaps from the water after crashing across a wave in the 1988 offshore Powerboat Grand Prix held in the Mediterranean off St Tropez. 5) The Italian ace powerboat man Renato Molinari steers his Martini Bianco Lancia 2100 horsepower craft through heavy seas off St Tropez during the 1988 offshore Powerboat Grand Prix. 6) The four-man *Annabella* leaps from the water during the 1988 World Powerboat Championships. 7) The Italian craft *Saima* leaves a wide wake during the 1988 World Powerboat Championships.

1

4. Jean-Marc Loubat

5. Y. Arthus Bertrand

2

6. Oli Tennent

7. Oli Tennent

1) Edoli of Italy taking part in the 1988 World Powerboat Championships. 2) The winged *Sandretto* craft surges through the water in the 1988 World Powerboat Championships. 3) The *Ellesse* crewed by the Monaco team of Casiraghi and Innocenti carves spray from the Mediterranean during the 1988 offshore race from Nice to Calvi. 4) A British powerboat races across the sea. The enormous thrusting energy of these racing craft has attained speeds of over 160 kilometres (100 miles) per hour during offshore races, though velocities of more than twice this have been recorded for special craft on smoothwater courses. 5) The Italian closed cockpit craft *Leader* competing in the 1988 Powerboat Grand Prix off St Tropez. 6) Adrian Ludin of France competing in the 1987 Paris 6 Hour Race. 7, 9, 10 & 11) Light outboard craft skim across the water, rather than driving through it, and are used only on sheltered inland waterways. 8) A Mitsubishi-sponsored craft flies across the water during the 1987 London Docks Grand Prix.

1. Oli Tennent

2. Oli Tennent

3. Gerard Vandystadt

4. Oli Tennent

5. Jean-Marc Loubat

6. Oli Tennent

7 Steve Powell

8. Oli Tennent

9. Steve Powell

10. Steve Powell

11. Steve Powell

1. Simon Ward

6

2. Simon Ward

Parachutes were first developed as a means of falling long distances and surviving, particularly from aircraft which got into difficulties. The parachute remained an emergency last resort for many years, though some early barnstormers used parachutes in their shows. Parachuting did not become accepted as a sport until after the Second World War when thousands of men had been trained in their use. Today skydiving is an established sport with accuracy and formation competitions being commonplace. 1) Skydivers attempting to form a star as they fall from a helicopter. 2) A stream of skydivers falling from a transport plane. 3) High-altitude skydivers form a three man ring. 4) A skydiving double act leaves the aircraft. 5) Vol Relatif takes up formation over Vichy in France. 6) Smoke canisters attached to the ankles of skydivers are often used during displays to mark the course of the falling parachutists. 7) A massive formation 'Relative Work' formed by several dozen skydivers.

3. Simon Ward

4. Simon Ward

5. F. Rickard/Artdiar

7

1. Guy Sauvage

2. Adrian Murrell

3. Philippe Moulu

1) The world record linked parachuting team of Voile Contact achieved by a French team in 1987. 2) The Australian Comb Services team preparing to link during a fall. 3) A modern micro-light aircraft and (4) a hang glider, both of which derive from the same space-age technology. A flexible wing formed from tough, man-made fabric stretched across a flexible metal leading edge was first developed in the 1950s but did not become viable for the general public until the early 1980s when technological advances made such light craft cheap enough for individual sportsmen. Hang gliding is now an established sport with thousands of adherents and well-organised international championships. 5) One of the more bizarre parachuting sports, the powered parachutist.

4. Didier Givois

5. Didier Givois

Until the 1980s the most used form of parachute was the circular silk parachute with a central hole which provided maximum stability in the fall, much needed when escaping from doomed aircraft. The introduction of the aerofoil-section rectangular parachute provided built-in instability which experienced jumpers could manipulate to control the direction and speed of their descent. 1) A pair of parachutists gently collide. 2) A column of 21 parachutists, the tallest column of the 1980s was one of 24 Royal Marines who successfully linked up in 1986. 3) A skydiver leaping from a balloon. The longest ever freefall was performed from a special high-altitude balloon by Captain Joe Kittinger of the US Airforce who fell 25 kilometres (16 miles) before opening his parachute. 4) A stack of parachutists. 5) An Alpine parachutist equipped with skis for a mountain landing.

1. Marcel Loli

2. Simon Ward

3. Simon Ward

4. Simon Ward

5. Bob Martin

Rallying may be loosely described as racing over roads rather than tracks, but most rallies are held on the kinds of roads most normal drivers would hesitate to negotiate in standard vehicles. The routes are designed to test the skills of the driver and robustness of the cars to the ultimate and involve dirt tracks, forestry paths and steep scrambles as well as normal road sections. 1) British driver Jonathan Palmer driving his Ford in the British Rally Cross. Palmer was better known as a Grand Prix driver but decided to try his hand at a different motoring sport. Unfortunately he failed in his bid to be become successful in two sports. 2) Stig Blomqvist of Sweden accelerates his Ford Sierra out of a wood during the 1987 R.A.C. Rally. 3) W. Rohrl negotiating a watersplash in his Audi 51. 4) The British driver Mark Rennington leads the field in his Ford RS 200 E in the 1988 British Rally on a section of dirt road. 5) Timo Salonen and Seppo Harjanne celebrating their victory in the 1986 R.A.C. Lombard Rally.

1. Pascal Rondeau

2. Oli Tennent

3. Bob Martin

4. Pascal Rondeau

5. Russell Cheyne

1. Russell Cheyne

2. Pascal Rondeau

3. Pascal Rondeau

Most modern rallies are held over a number of sections, each of which is timed and the times are added together at the close to decide on a winner. Early rallies, however, were not so sophisticated and were more in the style of straight races between two points. The greatest of the early rallies was the legendary Peking-Paris run of 12,000 kilometres (7,500 miles) which traversed territory so tough that only five entrants came forward. Of these only three completed the journey. 1) Stig Blomqvist of Sweden speeds along a muddy dirt track in the 1986 R.A.C. Rally. 2) B. Waldegard of Sweden splashes spectacularly through a ford in his Toyota on his way to gaining 3rd place in the 1988 Lombard R.A.C. Rally. 3) M. Sundstrom accelerates through a snow-bound Scottish forest during the 1988 R.A.C. Lombard Rally. 4) Timo Salonen kicks up dust during the 1988 R.A.C. Lombard Rally. 5) The Welsh driver with the Welsh name of David Llewelyn churns the mud on a forest section of the 1986 R.A.C. Rally.

4. Pascal Rondeau

5. Russell Cheyne

1. Yann Guichaoua

2. Y. Arthus Bertrand

3. Yann Guichaoua

4. Y. Arthus Bertrand

5. Maindru

6. Y. Arthus Bertrand

7. Maindru

8. Bob Snab

9. Yann Guichaoua

10. Maindru

11. Yann Guichaoua

1) Edi Orioli of Italy negotiates one of the desert stretches on the 1990 Paris-Dakar Rally which he went on to win. 2) One of the many backup trucks which followed the Paris-Dakar Rally in order to aid drivers if their vehicles broke down or if they needed assistance of any kind, including translation in conversations with locals. 3) The Italian rider Gualini on his Suzuki 750 racing across the Libyan desert during the 1990 Paris-Dakar Rally. 4) Herve Cotel of France powers out of a ford on the 1989 Paris-Tunis-Dakar Rally. 5) Herve Cotel on the 1990 Paris-Dakar Rally in his specially built 'Buggy Cotel'. 6) An Italian Lancia drives through a dust storm during the Kenya Rally. 7) Marrinoni of Italy wheelies his Yamaha YZE 750T bike during the 1990 Paris-Dakar Rally. 8) The Peugeot 405 Turbo 16 driven by Vatanen and Berglund on an early stage of the 1990 Paris-Dakar Rally. 9) A Mercedes 4x4 truck creates its own dust plume on the 1990 Paris-Dakar Rally. 10) Mas Samora of Spain speeds through the desert on his Yamaha YZE during the 1990 Paris-Dakar Rally. 11) Peugeot mechanics work during a night stop on the 1990 Paris-Dakar Rally.

1. J.P. Lenfant

2. Mike Powell

3. Mike Powell

Rodeo derives from the skills of the cowboys in the Old West of late last century when vast herds of cattle roamed the western plains of North America from the Gulf of Mexico to the Great Slave Lake. The cowboys would periodically gather together to compete in skill trials for which prizes of cash or equipment were on offer. Most of the events in modern rodeos are derived directly from necessary old skills. 1) Chuck wagon racing involves races between supply wagons and attendant outriders over a fixed course. 4) Calf-roping was carried out each summer to ensure that the calves were given the same brand of ownership as the mother cow for it was in this way that herds grew and were protected on the open range where cattle could mix freely. 6 & 7) Steer wrestling was used to bring an animal to a sudden stop. Steve Duhon (6) is the champion steer wrestler of the decade taking a string of titles. 8, 9 & 10) Bronc riding was a necessary skill in breaking wild horses to the saddle. 2, 3 & 5) Bull riding, however, was more of a joke event in the old days.

4. Mike Powell

5. Mike Powell

6. Mike Powell

7. Mike Powell

8. Mike Powell

9. Mike Powell

10. Dave Black

1) The men's coxed eights final in the 1985 World Rowing Championships. 2) The long, straight course of the Henley Regatta beneath the blazing sun which made the event particularly popular in 1989. It is the straight stretch of the Thames at Henley which ensured that the regatta first held in 1839 was held here and continues to be so. In the 150 years since it was founded, the Henley Regatta has developed into a great social event which draws thousands of visitors. 3) The British coxed eight team at the 1985 World Rowing Championships. 4) Two teams streak past the finishing line at the 1988 Henley Regatta. 5) Isis and Goldie, the junior crews from Oxford and Cambridge, on the Thames in 1986. 6) The coxless fours at 1985 the World Rowing Championships. 7) The Oxford-Cambridge boat race of 1986 which was won by Oxford and distinguished by the fact that the Cambridge crew included the youngest ever blue, Matthew Brittin aged 18 years.

1. Michael King

2. Joe Patronite

3. Michael King

6

4. Oli Tennent

5. Mike Powell

7

Rugby League as a distinct sport came into being in 1895 when the subject of amateurism split the main sporting body, not for the last time. The strictly amateur Rugby Union believed players should receive no payment while many northern clubs were in favour of paying players for loss of earnings incurred by playing. Agreement could not be reached so the northern clubs broke away to found the League which allowed for full-time paid players a few years later. The game has several differences from Rugby Union and is still a predominantly northern sport. 1) The referee has a word with the forwards during the 1987 Rugby League Final between Halifax and St Helens which ended in a 19-18 victory for the former. 2) A determined rush during the 18-10 defeat of Hull Kingston Rovers by Widness. 3) A diving tackle by Mick Scott brings a promising run by Ged Byrnie of Wigan to an end, but Wigan went on to gain a 32-12 victory. 4) Hull Kingston Rovers launch an abortive attack during the 1986 Challenge Cup which they lost 15-14. 5) Camelford celebrates its win in the 1986 Challenge Cup.

1. Bob Martin

2. Ben Radford

3. Simon Bruty

4. Mike King

5. Michael King

Rugby League playing rules have had an eventful history since the sport split away from Rugby Union in 1895. The number of players has been cut from 15 to 13 while there have been three successive changes in the scoring system which apportions different importance to tries, goals and conversions. The name Rugby League was not adopted until 1922, before that time the organisation had been known as the Northern Rugby Union, reflecting the games regional bias. 1) Wigan supporters joyfully cheer their team on at the Rugby League Cup Final of 1989 which was a virtual walkover for Wigan which beat St Helens 27-0. 2) The Widnes team poses for the cameramen after winning the 1989 Rugby League Charity Shield. 3) Halifax brings a run by Brendan Hill to a halt during the 1989-1990 Regal Trophy Final. 4) Halifax players grapple without success to halt a run by St Helens during the 1987 League Cup Final which resulted in a 19-18 win for Halifax. 5) A joyful Wigan player holds the Rugby League Cup after crushing St Helens 27-0 in the 1989 Final.

1. Michael King

2. Russell Cheyne

3. Phil Brown

4. Bob Martin

5. Ben Radford

Rugby Union traditionally began in November 1823 when a boy at Rugby School named William Ellis picked up the ball during a game of soccer. At this early date football was little developed from early rough games so such a tactic would not have been as revolutionary as it may appear. 1) The British Lions forwards attempt unsuccessfully to break through the Australian defence during the 3rd Test of the 1989 series. 2) Leaping Welsh players secure a high loose ball during their 24-15 victory over England on 20th April 1985. 3) Ireland on their way to a convincing 32-9 victory over Tonga in a play-off in the early stages of the first Rugby Union World Cup in 1987, which was contested between 16 nations. 4) A loose scrum during the tied match between France and Scotland with 20 points each at the Rugby World Cup of 1987. France went on to qualify but lost to the All Blacks in the final. 5) A United States forward falls prey to the English defence in the 34-6 English victory during the 1987 World Cup. 6) Teague and Dooley take a breather during the 3rd Test between Australia and the British Lions in 1989. 7) The Welsh team win the ball from the scrum during their 16-3 defeat of England during the Rugby World Cup of 1987. 8) A French forward passes the ball during the French 30-24 victory over Australia on their way to the final of the 1987 World Cup.

1. Billy Stickland

3. Mike Powell

2. Billy Stickland

4. Jean-Marc Barey

5. Russell Cheyne

6. Billy Stickland

1. Adrian Murrell

2. Billy Stickland

Rugby Union has successfully transplanted itself from its native home to nations around the World. The British Lions regularly tour around the world or host visiting teams from elsewhere. The international governing body of the sport was founded as early as the 1880s, at a time when many other sports were only just establishing national bodies. Since then international games have become increasingly frequent and popular. 1) The British Lions, a combined team of Welsh, English and Scots players, wins the ball from a tight scrum and kick into touch. 2) Wales wins the ball and passes it out to begin a long run during their 16-3 victory over England in the 1987 Rugby Union World Cup. 3) Iain Paxton runs with the ball, closely followed by a pack of players. 4) Mike Teague, later named player of the series, passes the ball out of a scrum to Robert Jones during the British Lions tour of Australia in 1989. 5) Nick Farr-Jones of Australia is tackled by Robert Jones of the British Lions at the moment of receiving a long pass during the 3rd Test between the two teams in 1989.

3. Michael King

4. Russell Cheyne

5. Billy Stickland

1. David Cannon

1) The forwards of France and Wales leap for the ball during a match which resulted in a 14-3 defeat for Wales. 2) Rodriguez launches an attack almost single-handed against the Welsh defence, streaking ahead of opposing players, during his teams 14-3 victory. 3) The French forwards prepare to lower their heads for a scrum during their 1989 victory over Scotland which had a final score line of 19-3. 4) David Kirk, captain of the New Zealand All Blacks, lifts the Rugby Union World Cup in triumph after leading his team to victory at the inaugural event in 1987. The magnificent All Blacks team beat France into second place with a thrilling match which ended with the convincing score line of 29 points to the All Blacks and 9 to France. 5) English players extricate the ball from a scrum on their way to defeating the United States by 34 points to 6 at the 1987 World Cup. Rugby Union is not particularly popular in the United States where American Football is the leading ball game and has already established itself.

2. David Cannon

3. Russell Cheyne

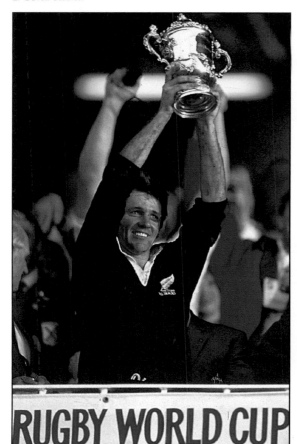

4. Jean-Marc Barey

5. Russell Cheyne

1) Competing yachts leave Southampton on the 2nd September 1989 for the start of the Whitbread Round the World Yacht Race, organised by the Royal Naval Sailing Association. The race is the longest in the world and is held every four years. Three official stops are allowed in the course of the race, at Cape Town, Auckland and in the River Plate and the entire race usually takes over four months to complete. 2) Sweden's *Royal Blue* leading other yachts in the 1987 Admiral's Cup. 3) Britain's *Young Endeavour* cruising through a gentle sea in the 1987 Admiral's Cup. 4) Jostling for position in the 1987 Admiral's Cup. 5) Colourful spinnaker sails set during a downwind run by contestants in the 1987 Admiral's Cup. The Admiral's Cup is the most competitive ocean yacht race with up to three vessels from any nation being allowed to compete. Though popular throughout the 1980s, the Admiral's Cup failed to attract the record field of 19 nations attained in 1979.

1. Philip Plisson

2. Oli Tennent

3. Oli Tennent

4. Oli Tennent

5. Oli Tennent

1. Bob Martin

2. Bob Martin

3. Emmanuel Zurini

4. Pascal Rondeau

5. Chris Cole

The Tall Ships Race brings together a number of old sailing ships from the era when the wind was all that propelled ships on their long trading voyages around the world. The graceful ships with their broad white sails make a magnificent show as they head out to sea for their strenuous race. Though elegant to the watcher, these big ships are immensely hard work to run. Each carries many miles of rigging, both standing and running, all of which has to be continually checked and adjusted as it is subjected to immense forces by the wind and waves. The ships are usually manned by naval volunteers or by voluntary organisations which keep the old craft in working order. The valuable craft are rarely risked in rough weather or dangerous waters. Most of the tall ships which compete are comparatively small trading ships dating from towards the end of the sail era. Larger ships are kept in dock. HMS *Victory* is the only surviving first rate wooden battleship and is preserved in dry-dock in Portsmouth, while the superbly fast clipper *Cutty Sark* is kept permanently moored where it is safe from storm and wreck.

1. Oli Tennent

2. Oli Tennent

3. Oli Tennent

4. Oli Tennent

7

5. Oli Tennent

1) A spinnaker sail comes down in a mass of fabric during the 1987 Admiral's Cup. Taking in a spinnaker is an art in ocean racing for although of immense use when running downwind, spinnakers can be tricky to handle in any other wind and if not stowed away quickly may lose the vessel valuable minutes in lost headway. 2 & 4) Crews take a rare breather from adjusting the sails as yachts race downwind in the 1987 Admiral's Cup. 3) *Jamerella* one of the British entries in the 1987 Admiral's Cup. 5) The Australian yacht *Sovereign* racing in the 1988 Kenwood Cup off Hawaii. 6) The British yacht *Indulgence* in the 1987 Admiral's Cup. 7) The start of the Ocean Triangle section of the 1988 Kenwood Cup. 8) *Il Moro* The Italian entry in the 1988 Kenwood Cup.

6. Oli Tennent

8

1. Allsport

2. Allsport

3. Kirk Schlea

4. Kirk Schlea

1) Two American yachts compete in 1986 to determine which should be the American challenger for the America's Cup. 2) Australian yachts *Kookaburra II* and *Kookaburra III* racing in 1986 to decide which would defend the America's Cup the following year. 3) The massive *New Zealand* dwarfs its crew as it races through the water. 4) The *Stars and Stripes* rests in harbour with the America's Cup in the foreground. The catamaran regained the America's Cup for the United States when it beat the *Kookaburra III* in four straight races off Perth in 1987. 5) Olivier Moussy of France skippers his catamaran. 6) The *Stars and Stripes*. 7) Preliminary races in the America's Cup competition off Fremantle in 1987. 8) The American *Jubilation* in the 1988 Kenwood Cup.

5. Bob Grieser

6. Philip Plisson

5. Trevor Jones

2. Jon Nicholson

3. Bob Martin

1. Jon Nicholson

4. John Gichigi

Competitions in horsemanship have been held for millennia. Most of these were designed to test the skills necessary for certain tasks performed on horseback. The rodeos of the American west contain competitions in calf-roping, wild-horse riding and wagon driving, all skills demanded during the working day of the cowboy. The equestrian sports as they exist today are derived from European riding schools of the 18th and 19th centuries where the gentry were taught to tackle the jumps and obstacles they might encounter when riding as a form of transport. 1) Eddie Macken, a popular rider with the audiences, jumps in an attempt to win the 1989 Dubai Cup. 2) Tony Newbery stands in his stirrups as he clears a fence in the Dubai Cup of 1989. 3) Harvey Smith clears a fence on Sanyo Shining Example at the 1987 Windsor Horse Show. Smith was possibly the most controversial rider of the decade. He renamed all his horses in a sponsorship deal with the Japanese electronics company Sanyo and ran into repeated and much reported controversies with umpires and judges. 4) Graham Fletcher rides his grey Stylo Wilkie over a fence at Hickstead in 1989. 5) American rider Conrad Homfeld riding at the 1984 Los Angeles Olympics. 6) Malcolm Pyrah on Sea Pearl clears a combination wall and diagonal pole. 7) Harvey Smith on Sanyo Shining Example at the 1987 Windsor Horse Show.

5. Trevor Jones

3. Bob Martin

1) Robert Smith on Silver Dust jumping in the 1989 Hickstead Jumping Derby. 2) Lucinda Green, previously better known under her maiden name of Lucinda Prior-Palmer, riding in the 1984 Olympic Games. 3) The British rider Geoff Glazzard riding Kliekilink at the 1987 Windsor Horse Show. 4) Paddy MacMahon on Toyota Tigre in 1982. Steep banks and other earthen obstacles have become common hazards on outdoor show jumping circuits. They provide novel entertainment for the crowd and face horse and rider with demanding feats of jumping. None of these, however, matches up to the obstacles posed at military riding schools in the last century where horse and rider were trained for battlefield conditions. The famed Prussian riding school final course included a sheer drop of over 20 metres (60 feet) down which cavalry men were expected to ride their mounts. 5) Nick Skelton on Everest Arabesque. 6) Paddy MacMahon setting Toyota Tigre at a more conventional show jumping fence. 7) Malcolm Pyrah on Its Me at the Windsor Horse Show in 1987.

1

4. Bob Martin

5. Trevor Jones

2

6. Tony Duffy

7. Bob Martin

1. Kit Houghton

2. John Gichigi

3. Bob Martin

4. Simon Bruty

5. Bob Martin

7

1) Cynthia Oshuy rides Dynasty for Canada in the dressage event at the Seoul Olympics. 2) Annette Lewis on Zephyrus at Hickstead in 1989. 3) Derek Ricketts rides Lorisking down a steep bank with consumate ease in September 1981. 4) Murphy Himself gallops through the water course at the Badminton Horse Trials. 5) A steep earthen bank tackled in classic fashion by leaning back in the stirrups and allowing the horse to slide down the slope on its haunches. 6) Prince Philip, Duke of Edinburgh, guides his four in hand team during the Brighton Driving Trials. 7) Australian trotting horses. Light harness racing is divided in two categories according to the gait of the horse. Trotters use diagonally opposite legs simultaneously while pacers have both legs on each side of the body working together. 8) Argentinian horsemen engaging in a game of pato. Played with a large ball to which are attached loops of strings so that riders can grasp it easily the game may date back to ancient equestrian games played on the Eurasian steppes by nomadic horse-warriors of Genghis Khan.

6. David Cannon

8

1. Steve Powell

2. Guido Benetton

3. Guido Benetton

4. Guido Benetton

1

5. Steve Powell

6. David Cannon

2

7. Guido Benetton

Easily the most efficient method of travelling over snow is by the use of skis. On level stretches the skier pushes himself along with sticks and allows gravity to do its work on downhill runs. The oldest known skis in the world were dug out of a peat bog in Sweden and tentatively dated to before 2,000 BC. The earliest sporting ski competitions were also held in Scandinavia in the mid-19th century. 1) The great Franz Klammer of Austria turns in a high speed donwhill run. Klammer has taken 5 World Cup titles in the downhill events and won over two dozen individual races. 2) Marc Girardelli of Luxembourg competing in a slalom contest during the 1988-1989 season. 3) Daniel Mahrer of Switzerland skims over powder snow in 1988. 4) Armin Bittner leans into a turn as he competes in the 1988 World Cup. 5) Doug Lewis in an untidy leap during the Montana Championships of 1987. 6) The Swiss skier P. Zurbriggen leaps past a gate in the slalom event at the 1988 Calgary Winter Olympics. 7) Peter Mueller of Switzerland in a downhill event in 1988.

1. Steve Powell

2. Steve Powell

3. David Cannon

Skiing as a sport rather than a form of transport did not become properly established until the close of the last century. Nordic skiing was organised first with downhill skiing waiting until the 1920s by which time efficient mechanical lifts had been invented. 1) A colourfully clad P. Zurbriggen of Switzerland clips a gate during a slalom event. 2) The Italian skier Alberto Tomba who is a well known and athletic slalom skier. 3) Marc Girardelli of Luxembourg throws up a shower of snow in the giant slalom event at Crans Montana in 1987. 4) Alberto Tomba skiing his way to a gold medal in the men's giant slalom at the Calgary Winter Olympic Games in 1988. 5) P. Zurbriggen skims past a gate in his bronze-medal-winning run at the 1988 Calgary Winter Olympics. 6) Ingemar Stenmark of Sweden competing in the 1988 Calgary Winter Olympics. Stenmark has had a remarkable career, winning 8 slalom and 7 giant slalom World Cup titles. 7) Robert Zan of Yugoslavia at the 1987 Crans Montana. 8) Ingemar Stenmark of Sweden almost loses control in 1988.

4. David Cannon

5. David Cannon

6. David Cannon

1. David Cannon

2. David Cannon

3. Guido Benetton

4. Yann Guichaoua

1) P. Dupasquier of Switzerland leaves the snow during an exceptionally speedy downhill run. 2) Carole Merle of France steadying herself on a tight corner during a long run. 3) The Canadian skier Karen Percy slips around a gate pole during a thrilling slalom run in 1988. 4) Disaster is imminent for Maria Birkner of Argentina in the women's giant slalom event at the 1988 Calgary Winter Olympic Games when her ski gets entangled with a slalom gate and ripped from her feet. Seconds later she tumbled to the ground, thus ending her bid for a medal in ignominious fashion. 5) Gilli-Bruegger of Switzerland setting out on the women's 20 kilometre Nordic ski race at the 1988 Calgary Winter Olympics. Nordic racing, with its cross country route and uphill sections as well as downhill runs, is more closely linked to the original use of skis for transport than are the thrilling downhill Alpine events.

5. Gray Mortimore

1) Villard de Lans of France displays his specialised speed skiing equipment. Speed skiing concentrates on velocity rather than agility and demands peculiar equipment including streamlined helmets, leg fins and aerodynamic gauntlets as shown here. 2) Jan Bucher snaps an unusual photo using a camera tied to the sticks while hot-dogging during the Skiing World Championships of 1986. 3) Lillehammer of Norway setting out on the men's biathlon at the 1987 World Championships. The biathlon combines the disciplines of skiing and shooting and is particularly popular with the military. 4) The Swedish skier Majback striding out to win the 1989 World Championships team Nordic event. 5) The new sport of snow-surfing in spectacular action as a proficient surfer in shorts more suited to sea surfing in Hawaii than snow-surfing in Switzerland leaps over a mound and loses contact with his dog. 6) The crowded ski run at Tignes-Alpes in France during the winter of 1985-1986.

1. Jean-Marc Barey

2. Bob Martin

3. Jean-Marc Barey

4. Pascal Rondeau

5. Jean-Marc Barey

6. Gerard Vandystadt

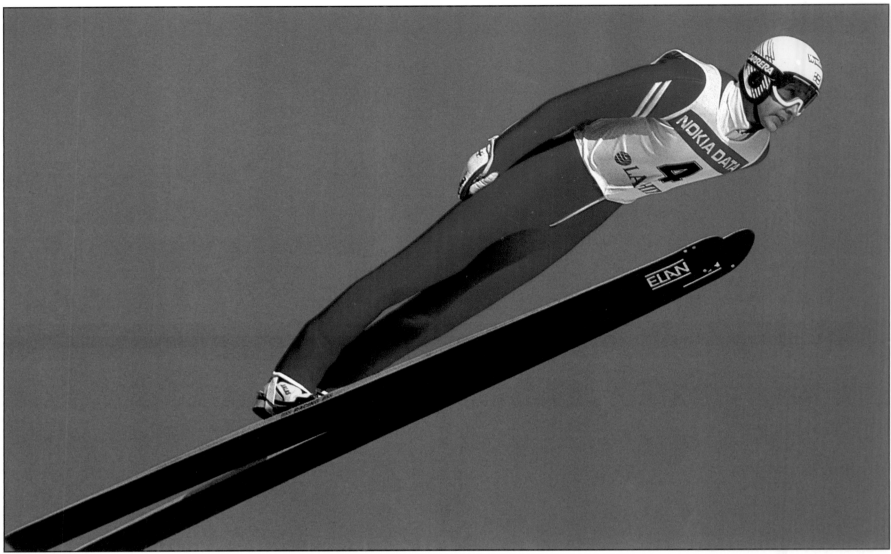

1. Guido Benetton

2. Yann Guichaoua

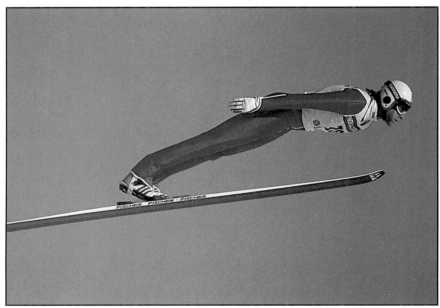

3. Pascal Rondeau

4. Pascal Rondeau

5. Yann Guichaoua

6. Pascal Rondeau

7. Pascal Rondeau

1) Matti Nykanen of Finland who won the World Championship in 1989 and is widely regarded as the greatest ski-jumper of the late 1980s. 2) The Norwegian H. Bogseth leaping from the 70 metre ski jump at the 1988 Calgary Winter Olympic Games. 3) Dieter Thoma spreads his arms to steady his flight as his skis slide apart at the 1989 World Ski Championships. 4) Czech ski-jumper M. Svagerko displays a near perfect leaping position at the 1989 World Ski Championships. 5) Austria's H. Aschenwald leaps from the 70 metre ski jump at the 1988 Calgary Winter Olympic Games. 6) A contestant hurtles down the long slope to the ski-jump take-off point along ruts worn by many skiers before him at the World Ski Championships of 1989. 7) A competitor launches into air from the base of the ski jump at the 1989 World Ski Championships. The massive height of the ski jump can be properly appreciated in this shot. 8) Obersdorf leaps from the 70 metre ski-jump at the 1987 World Ski Championships in a suit which owes much to abstract modern art. 9) Pavel Ploc of Czechoslovakia leaping into 4th place, and narrowly missing a medal, on the 90 metre ski-jump at the 1988 Calgary Winter Olympic Games. 10) Matti Nykanen leaping to victory in the 90 metre ski-jump at the 1984 Winter Olympic Games. 11) Eddie Edwards of Great Britain leaping into the newspapers at the 70 metre ski-jump at the Calgary Winter Olympics. The cheerfully amateur skier became immensely popular although he finished in last place.

9. Jean-Marc Barey

8. Gerard Vandystadt

10. Steve Powell

11. Gray Mortimore

1. Pascal Rondeau

2. Adrian Murrell

1) Alex 'Hurricane' Higgins lines up to pot a red during the 1988 World Snooker Championships. Higgins gained his soubriquet from his lightning speed at the table seeming barely to pause between taking shots which he potted with almost unfailing dexterity. 2) Steve Davis with the silver cup for which he was playing at the 1986 World Championships. 3) Dennis Taylor lining up to pot a high-scoring break during his historic tussle with Steve Davis in the 1985 World Snooker Championships. 4) Steve Davis and John Parrot shake hands at the 1989 World Snooker Final. 5) Steve Davis concentrates on a vital shot at the 1987 World Snooker Championships. 6) Dennis Taylor chalks his cue while studying the layout of balls during a match in the 1988 World Snooker Championships. 7) Steve Davis at the 1989 World Championships. 8) Terry Griffith at the 1987 World Snooker Championships. 9) The youthful Stephen Hendry lines up a red at the 1988 World Snooker Championships. 10) 'Whirlwind' Jimmy White in action at the 1988 World Snooker Championships. 11) Cliff Thorburn studiously lines up a shot at the 1988 World Snooker Championships.

3. Adrian Murrell

4. Gray Mortimore

5. Bob Martin

6. Pascal Rondeau

7. Gray Mortimore

8. Trevor Jones

9. Pascal Rondeau

10. Pascal Rondeau

11. Pascal Rondeau

1. Tony Duffy

2. Bob Martin

Humans have been able to swim since time immemorial but racing did not become an established sport until early in the last century when interest in sports of many different kinds increased dramatically. 1) Adrian Moorhouse of Great Britain raises his arms to celebrate taking the gold medal in the 100 metres breaststroke at the 1988 Seoul Olympic Games. 2) Andrew Jameson powers through the water in the butterfly finals of the United States Championships of 1986. 3) The distinctive figure of Duncan Goodhew launches himself from the diving block at the start of the 100 metres breaststroke final at the 1980 Moscow Olympic Games at which he won the gold medal. 4) The white-capped head of Great Britain's Nick Gillingham lifts as he surges through the water at the 1989 European Swimming Championships on his way to equalling the world record for the 200 metre breast-stroke. 5) A glittering stream at the backstroke finals in the 1987 European Championships.

3. Tony Duffy

4. Simon Bruty

5. Simon Bruty

1. Mike King

2. Jean-Marc Barey

3. Tony Duffy

4. Simon Bruty

5. Tony Duffy

6. Tony Duffy

Though swimming comes naturally not all strokes were developed at once. Until the 18th century the breast-stroke was the most popular in Europe. Then sailors brought back the crawl they had seen used by the South Sea Islanders and the breast-stroke was edged out of popularity. 1) Michael Gross of West Germany churns the water in a butterfly race, the stroke with which he won both 100 metre and 200 metre European championships. 2) The start of the women's final at the 1986 World Swimming Championships held in Madrid. 3) The start of the men's final at the 1986 World Swimming Championships in Madrid. 4) Adrian Moorhouse comes up for air as he powers through the water at the 1989 European Swimming Championships to break the world record for the 100 metre breast-stroke. 5) Alexandra Worisch breaks the surface in dynamic fashion during the 1981 European Swimming Championships. 6) Tracy Caulkins of the United States.

1. Steve Powell

2. Chris Cole

3. Chris Cole

The game generally referred to as tennis is in fact the outdoor version of real tennis and is more properly termed lawn tennis. Real tennis originated in the dark ages as a game played by monks in the cloisters of their monasteries. It was later adopted by the nobility and became a highly fashionable game. Lawn tennis developed around the middle of the 19th century with the rules of real tennis being considerably altered to take account of the lack of walls and roofs. The game quickly caught on and by the end of the century international competitions were being held. 1) The great Bjorn Borg of Sweden serves at the 1980 Wimbledon Championships where he broke all records by achieving a fifth consecutive victory in the men's singles final. He announced his retirement from top standard tennis soon afterward. 2) The young German star Boris Becker stretches for a shot at the 1987 Stella Artois Trophy. 3) Jimmy Connors plays his famous two-handed backhand during the 1987 U.S. Open by which time he was beginning to be overshadowed by new young players. 4) A hot Jimmy Connors stretches desperately for a wide ball at the 1988 Liptons' Championship in Florida. 5) Boris Becker lifts his arms in the air as the crowd explodes into applause to celebrate his winning of the men's singles final at Wimbledon in 1985 to become the youngest ever title-holder at the age of just 17 years old. 6) Boris Becker playing at Wimbledon in 1989.

4. Bob Martin

5. Trevor Jones

1. Steve Powell

2. Bob Martin

3. Bob Martin

1) John McEnroe leaps to play a ball during the 1984 Wimbledon Championships. McEnroe dominated the tennis headlines throughout much of the decade. Not only was his tennis inspired and brilliant, but his volatile temperament embroiled him in a succession of disputes with umpires and referees. The stark contrast between his amazing playing abilities and his brash manner set McEnroe on a switchback ride of popularity with the public as he received alternating cheers and boos at his various appearances. 2) Mats Wilander at the French Open. 3) Stefan Edberg collapses to the ground after playing the winning shot at the 1988 Wimbledon to take the men's singles title for the first time. 4) The tennis sensation of 1989 was the diminutive Michael Chang of the United States who beat many of the great players and stormed his way through numerous qualifying rounds to establish himself as a rising star of the future.

4. Ch. Petit/Gerard Vandystadt

1) Boris Becker of West Germany clinches a vital point at the 1986 Wimbledon Championship as he attempts to repeat his startling success in the men's singles event of the previous year. 2) The highly popular Australian player Pat Cash hits a winning shot while wearing his distinctive headband which became something of a personal trademark over the decade. 3) Pat Cash stretches for a low base shot during the 1987 Wimbledon men's singles final. When he won the championship, Cash won many hearts by immediately dashing into the crowd and clambering over the seats to join his family and friends before returning to the court for the formal presentation of the trophy by the Duke of Kent. 4) Yannick Noah of France sprints to reach a ball during the 1987 French Open Tournament. 5) Ivan Lendl celebrates a triumph over Boris Becker at the 1989 Wimbledon Championships. 6) John McEnroe gives a whoop of joy before falling to his knees after playing the winning shot of the 1981 Wimbledon men's singles final and so taking the title for the first time. 7) The American player Andre Agassi plays in informal wear at the 1988 Liptons' Championships in Florida. The various championships have different dress regulations with Wimbledon insisting on predominantly white outfits.

1. Steve Powell

2. Allsport

3. Chris Cole

4. Chris Cole

5. Bob Martin

6. Tony Duffy

7. Bob Martin

1) Steffi Graff, the rising young star of West German women's tennis in the latter part of the decade, playing in the 1987 French Open which she won in the following year. 2) The Spanish player Sanchez prepares to power a backhand shot across the court during the 1989 French Open. 3) Martina Navratilova reaches for a fast ball during a match at Wimbledon in 1987. In that year she won her eighth women's singles title, having previously won in 1978, 1979, 1982, 1983, 1984, 1985 and 1986. She thus equalled the long standing record of Helen Moody who completed her eighth successful championship 49 years earlier. 4) Chris Evert readies herself to slam a forehand pass across the court at the 1989 Liptons Championship in Florida. 5) Steffi Graff throws the ball for her first service during the 1987 French Open Championship. 6) Chris Evert waves goodbye to her many fans on leaving the court at Wimbledon after playing her final singles match at the tournament on the 6th July 1989. 7) The Yugoslavian player Monica Seles leaps to reach an awkward ball during the 1989 Roland Garros.

1. Chris Cole

2. Simon Bruty

3. Chris Cole

4. Bob Martin

5. Chris Cole

6. Bob Martin

7. Ch. Petit/G. Vandystadt

1. Bob Martin

2. Bob Martin

4. Chris Cole

1) Gabriella Sabatini of Argentina playing in the 1987 French Open. The rise to world prominence of the young Argentinian was accompanied by a scramble among sports sponsors to gain her favour for the winning personality and good looks of the star made her a natural television and press personality. 2) Chris Evert of the United States watches the progress of a winning forehand drive at the Liptons' Championship in Florida. Chris Evert dominated the women's game for much of the decade but abandoned world class tennis as the 1980s closed. 3) Steffi Graf of West Germany playing at the 1988 Liptons' Championship in Florida. 4) Martina Navratilova playing in the 1987 French Open. It is generally estimated that Navratilova has earned more money from tennis than any other woman with her total earnings estimated at up to around $15 million.

3. Bob Martin

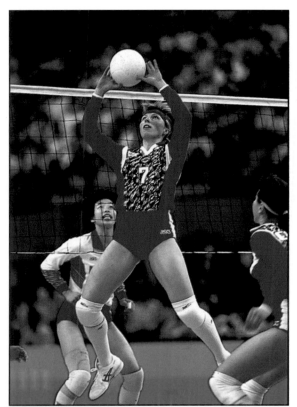

1. Bruce Hazleton

2. Trevor Jones

3. Bruce Hazleton

4. Mike Powell

1) Irena Parkhomtchouk leaps to thrust the ball over the net to the Japanese team during the final match of the women's volleyball in the 1988 Seoul Olympics in which Russia took the gold medal, leaving the silver to the Japanese. 2) The 1984 victory by the United States over Tunisia. 3) A United States player leaps to send an overhead smash into the Russian court in the men's final at the Seoul Olympics. The United States won the match and took the gold medals home across the Pacific. 4) Eric Ngapeth of France punches a ball at two Russian players during the U.S.A. Cup. 5) The Korean women's team at the Olympic Games. 6) A Brazilian player delivers an overhead smash at Argentina in 1984. 7) Craig Buck of the United States serves to Canada during the U.S.A. Cup. 8) Holland losing to the United States in the 1988 Seoul Olympics. 9) An American player delivers a winning shot to the Japanese team during he 1988 Seoul Olympics. 10) Mierya Luis Scores a point against the United States during the 1987 Pan-American Games. 11) The United States beating Korea in 1984.

5. Bruce Hazleton

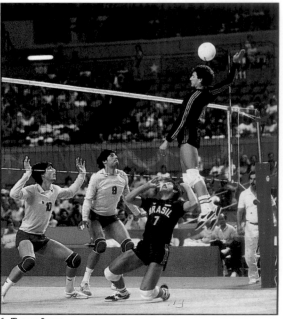

6. Trevor Jones

7. Mike Powell

8. Bruce Hazleton

9. Tony Duffy

10. Bruce Hazleton

11. Trevor Jones

1. Steve Powell

5

2. David Cannon

3. Michael King

Water Polo is one of the oldest water sports, except for race swimming. It was first developed in English public schools in the 1860s where sport of all kinds, and team sports in particular, were considered essential to the character development of young gentlemen. The sport gained rapidly in popularity and has been an internationally contested sport throughout the entire 20th century. 2) The Italian team playing Canada at the 1984 Los Angeles Olympics. 3) A goal is scored during the 1985 European Championships. 4) A struggle for the ball produces rough water during the French Championships. 5) The United States plays Cuba in the Pan-American Games of 1979. 6) A shot at goal during a match between the United States and Italy.

4. Patrick Vielcanet

6

1) Andrea Alessi of Italy at the European Waterskiing Championships. 2) Cutting a dash on a single ski. 3) Patrice Martin of France creates a curtain of spray during the World Waterskiing Championships held at Toulouse in 1985. 4) Britt Larson of the United States executing a trick step at the World Waterskiing Championships of 1987. 5) Bob LaPoint of the United States at the 1987 World Waterskiing Championships. 6) A curtain of water created by a single-ski waterskier. 7) Yvon Legali of France sweeps wide during the European Waterskiing Championships while holding the bar with only one hand. 8) Camille Dovall of the United States leans back to gather speed to cross the wake during the 1987 World Waterskiing Championships. 9) Mike Neville of Australia at the 1987 World Waterskiing Championships.

1. Gray Mortimore

2. Allen Steele

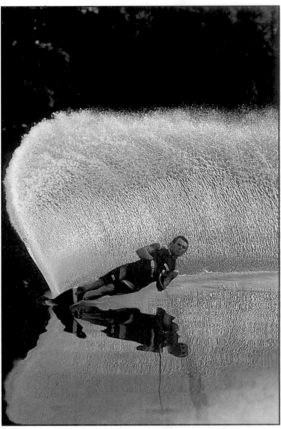

3. Jean-Marc Barey

4. Oli Tennent

5. Oli Tennent

6. Allen Steele

7. Gray Mortimore

8. Oli Tennent

9. Oli Tennent

1. Russell Cheyne

2. Gray Mortimore

3. Gray Mortimore

4. David Cannon

5. Russell Cheyne

6. David Cannon

7. David Cannon

8. Simon Bruty

9. Mike Powell

10. David Cannon

11. Gerard Vandystadt

Weight-lifting was largely confined to circuses and street shows until the 1890s when properly organised competitions began. 1) A. Khrapatyzi of the USSR lifting 225 kilograms at the 1988 Seoul Olympics. 2) The Russian weight-lifter Israil Arsamakov winning the light heavyweight title at the 1988 Seoul Olympics. 3) Karen Marshall of the United States setting a new World Record for the snatch in the women's over 82.5 kilogram category. 4) Bartholomew Duoma lifting 150 kilograms in August 1984. 5) The Polish weight-lifter A. Piotrowski attempts to lift a 200 kilogram weight at the 1988 Seoul Olympics. 6) David Mercer of Great Britain winning the bronze medal in the middle-heavyweight category in 1984. 7) Manfred Nerlinger of West Germany fails in a lift at the Los Angeles Olympics of 1984. 8) Huan Ming of Vietnam strains during his bronze-medal-winning lift at the 1988 Seoul Olympics in the featherweight class. 9) A successful lift in the Seoul Olympics. 10) Lee Minwoog of Korea begins his winning lift in the heavyweight class. 11) Tsai Wen-Yee collapses after failing to make a lift.

1. Agence Vandystadt

2. Jean-Marc Barey

3. Jean-Marc Barey

4. Didier Givois

White water was previously counted a deadly hazard to rafts, so much so that travellers would carry their raft and its contents overland rather than risk disaster. However, the development of tough and durable inflatable rafts made it possible to tackle even the most formidable white water runs with a degree of safety and a new sport was born. 1) Paddling an inflatable raft through a mountain gorge. 2) The 1985 Rafting Championships held on the Isere River in France. 3) The five man inflatable raft which is favoured by many white-water rafters. 4) The 'Dora Baltea' is lifted upwards by a massive wave while rafting down an Alpine gorge in Italy. 5) Rafting in France. 6) A five man raft is followed down the Isere by a kayak during the 1985 Rafting Championships held on the Isere River in France. 7) Kayaks and rafts on the Isere in France. 8) A raft ploughs into a standing wave on the Isere in France. 9) The view from the rear of a tourist raft as it approaches a stretch of white water.

5. Jean-Marc Barey

6. Jean-Marc Barey

7. Agence Vandystadt

8. Jean-Marc Barey

9. Ed Blankman

1. Agence Vandystadt

2. Oli Tennent

3. Jon Nicholson

4. Christian Petit

7

5. Jon Nicholson

The great new sport of the 1980s was windsurfing which built on a rapidly gained popularity in the 1970s to become an Olympic sport by the close of the decade. 1) The French windsurfer Pascal Maka who holds the world record for speed on a windsurf board at 38 knots (71 kilometres per hour). 2) Pacal Maka competing in the speed trials during Weymouth Week in 1987. 3) An athletic leap during the 1988 Windsurfing Championships. 4) Robby Naish of the United States windsurfing his way to his third consecutive World Championship in 1985. 5) A leap off the Californian coast where the sport of windsurfing began. 6) The colourful underside of an Australian windsurfer's board. 7) Windsurfers racing offshore. 8) A group of windsurfers. The clear plastic patches on the sails are essential to the windsurfer as they enable him to see approaching craft.

6. Jon Nicholson

8

3. Agence Vandystadt

4. Simon Dargoud

5. Jon Nicholson

6. Agence Vandystadt

Surfing was a traditional sport of the Polynesian islanders who delighted in riding the large Pacific rollers to the shores of their island homes. The pastime was commented upon by all early European visitors but did not catch on as a sport with Europeans until new styles of board construction in the 1920s. 1) Riding a pipeline, that is surfing within the breaking wave, on the coast of Hawaii. 2) Windsurfing towards the breakers. 3) A spectacular windsurfing leap. 4) Windsurfers in a quiet cove. 5) A lone windsurfer on a late afternoon. 6) Land yachting in 1985 by which time land yachters had adopted a wheeled version of the windsurf board rather than the older yacht-rigged carriages. 7) The 1988 Windsurfing Championships. 8) A windsurfer leaps.

1

7. Jon Nicholson

8. Jon Nicholson

2